From

CW00613333

Welcome to our extra-spec
astrological forecast which ta
up to the end of the century on December 31, ~~~~

our year-ahead guides all the astrological calculations had to be made using
tables and a calculator. Today, by the miracle of computers, we have been able
to build our knowledge and hard work into a program which calculates the
precise astrological aspect for every day in a flash.

When Shakespeare wrote 'The fault, dear Brutus, is not in our stars, but in
ourselves', he spoke for every astrologer. In our day-to-day forecasts we
cannot hope to be 100% accurate every time, because this would remove the
most important influence in your life, which is you! What we can hope to do
is to give you a sense of the astrological backdrop to the day, week or month
in question, and so prompt you to think a little harder about what is going in
your own life, and thus help improve your chances of acting effectively to deal
with events and situations.

During the course of a year, there may be one or two readings that are
similar in nature. This is not an error, it is simply that the Moon or a planet
has repeated a particular pattern. In addition, a planetary pattern that applies
to your sign may apply to someone else's sign at some other point during the
year. One planetary 'return' that you already know well is the Solar return
that occurs every year on your birthday.

If you've read our guides before, you'll know that we're never less than
positive and that our advice is unpretentious, down to earth, and rooted in
daily experience. If this is the first time you've met us, please regard us not
as in any way astrological gurus, but as good friends who wish you nothing
but health, prosperity and contentment. Happy 1998-9!

Sasha Fenton is a world-renowned astrologer, palmist and Tarot card reader, with over 80 books published on Astrology, Palmistry, Tarot and other forms of divination. Now living in London, Sasha is a regular broadcaster on radio and television, as well as making frequent contributions to newspapers and magazines around the world, including South Africa and Australia. She is a former President and Secretary of the British Astrological and Psychic Society (BAPS) and Secretary of the Advisory Panel on Astrological Education.

Jonathan Dee is an astrologer, artist and historian based in Wales, and a direct descendant of the great Elizabethan alchemist and wizard Dr John Dee, court astrologer to Queen Elizabeth I. He has written a number of books, including the recently completed *The Chronicles of Ancient Egypt,* and for the last five years has co-written an annual astrological forecast series with Sasha Fenton. A regular broadcaster on television and radio, he has also hosted the Starline show for KQED Talk Radio, New Mexico.

YOUR DAY-BY-DAY FORECAST
SEPTEMBER 1998 – DECEMBER 1999

SASHA FENTON • JONATHAN DEE

HALDANE • MASON

Zambezi

DEDICATION
For the memory of Gary Bailey, a new star in heaven.

ACKNOWLEDGEMENTS
With many thanks to our computer wizard, Sean Lovatt.

This edition published 1998
by Haldane Mason Ltd
59 Chepstow Road
London W2 5BP

ISBN 1-902463-06-4

Designed and produced by Haldane Mason Ltd
Cover illustration by Lo Cole
Edited by Jan Budkowski

Printed in Singapore by Craft Print Pte Ltd

CONTENTS

AN ASTROLOGICAL OVERVIEW OF THE 20TH CENTURY   6

THE ESSENTIAL AQUARIUS   16

YOUR SUN SIGN   20

ALL THE OTHER SUN SIGNS   21

YOU AND YOURS   29

YOUR RISING SIGN   36

AQUARIUS IN LOVE   41

YOUR PROSPECTS FOR 1999   43

AQUARIUS IN THE FINAL QUARTER OF 1998   46

AQUARIUS IN 1999   70

An Astrological Overview of the 20th Century

Next year the shops will be full of astrology books for the new century and also for the new millennium. In this book, the last of the old century, we take a brief look back to see where the slow-moving outer planets were in each decade and what it meant. Obviously this will be no more than a very brief glance backwards but next year you will be able to see the picture in much more depth when we bring out our own book for the new millennium.

1900 – 1909

The century began with Pluto in Gemini and it was still in Gemini by the end of the decade. Neptune started out in Gemini but moved into cancer in 1901 and ended the decade still in Cancer. Uranus started the century in Sagittarius, moving to Capricorn in 1904 and ending the decade still in Capricorn. Saturn began the century in Sagittarius, moving to Capricorn in January 1900 and then through Aquarius, Pisces and Aries, ending the decade in Aries.

The stars and the decade

In general terms, the planet of upheaval in the dynastic sign of Sagittarius with Saturn also in that sign and Pluto opposing it, all at the very start of the century put the spotlight on dynasties, royalty and empires. As Saturn left for the 'establishment' sign of Capricorn these just about held together but as the decade ended, the power and control that these ancient dynasties had were loosening their grip on the developed world of the time. Queen Victoria died in 1901 and her son, Edward VII was dying by the end of the decade, so in Britain, the Victorian age of certainty was already coming to an end. The Boer War was only just won by Britain in 1902 which brought a shock to this successful colonial country.

Pluto in Gemini brought a transformation in methods of communications. It was as Saturn entered the innovative sign of Aquarius that these took concrete and useful form. Thus it was during this decade that the motor car, telephone, typewriter, gramophone and colour photography came into existence. Air travel began in 1900 with the first Zeppelin airship flight, the first powered aeroplane flight by the Wright brothers in 1904 and Louis Blériot's flight across the English Channel in 1909. Edison demonstrated the Kinetophone, the first machine capable of showing talking moving pictures in

1910. Even the nature of war changed as technologically modern Japan managed to fight off the might of the Russian empire in the war of 1904 - 1905.

The Treaty of Versailles, followed by further treaties of Aix and Trianon served to crush the German nation and therefore sow the seeds of the next war.

1910 - 1919

Pluto opened the decade in Gemini, moving to Cancer in 1913. Neptune travelled from Cancer to Leo in September 1914 while Uranus moved out of Capricorn, through Aquarius to end the decade in Pisces. Saturn moved from Aries to Taurus, then to Gemini, back into Taurus, then into Gemini again entering Cancer in 1914, then on through Leo and ending the decade in Virgo.

The stars and the decade

Now we see the start of a pattern. Sagittarius may be associated with dynasties but it is the home-loving and patriotic signs of Cancer and Leo that actually seem to be associated with major wars. The desire either to expand a country's domestic horizons or to protect them from the expansion of others is ruled by the maternal sign of Cancer, followed by the paternal one of Leo. Home, family, tradition, safety all seem to be fought over when major planets move through these signs. When future generations learn about the major wars of the 20th century they will probably be lumped together in their minds - despite the 20-year gap between them - just as we lump the Napoleonic wars together, forgetting that there was a nine-year gap between them, and of course, this long stay of Pluto in Cancer covered the whole of this period.

It is interesting to note that Pluto moved into Cancer in July 1913 and Neptune entered Leo on the 23rd of September 1914, just three of weeks after the outbreak of the First World War. Saturn moved into Cancer in April 1914. Pluto is associated with transformation, Neptune with dissolution and Saturn with loss, sadness and sickness. Many people suffered and so many families and dynasties were unexpectedly dissolved at that time, among these, the Romanov Czar and his family and the kings of Portugal, Hungary, Italy and Germany and the Manchu dynasty of China. America (born on the 4th of July, 1776 and therefore a Cancerian country) was thrust into prominence as a major economic and social power after this war. Russia experienced the Bolshevik revolution during it. As Saturn moved into Virgo (the sign that is associated with health) at the end of this decade, a world-wide plague of influenza killed 20 million people, far more than had died during the course of the war itself.

1920 – 1929

The roaring 20s began and ended with Pluto in Cancer. Neptune moved from Leo to Virgo at the end of this decade and Uranus moved from Pisces to Aries in 1927. Saturn travelled from Virgo, through Libra, Scorpio, Sagittarius and then backwards and forwards between Sagittarius and Capricorn, ending up in Capricorn at the end of 1929.

The stars and the decade

Pluto's long transformative reign in Cancer made life hard for men during this time. Cancer is the most female of all the signs, being associated with nurturing and motherhood. Many men were sick in mind and body as a result of the war and women began to take proper jobs for the first time. Family planning and better living conditions brought improvements in life for ordinary people and in the developed world there was a major boom in house building as well as in improved road and rail commuter systems. The time of lords and ladies was passing and ordinary people were demanding better conditions. Strikes and unrest were common, especially in Germany. As the decade ended, the situation both domestically and in the foreign policies of the developed countries began to look up. Even the underdeveloped countries began to modernize a little. Shortly before the middle of this decade, all the politicians who might have prevented the rise of Hitler and the Nazi party died and then came the stock market crash of 1929. The probable astrological sequence that set this train of circumstances off was the run up to the opposition of Saturn in Capricorn to Pluto in Cancer which took place in 1931. The effects of such major planetary events are often felt while the planets are closing into a conjunction or opposition etc., rather than just at the time of their exactitude.

On a brighter note great strides were made in the worlds of art, music and film and ordinary people could enjoy more entertainment than ever before, in 1929 the first colour television was demonstrated and in 1928 Alexander Fleming announced his discovery of penicillin. At the very start of the decade prohibition passed into US Federal law, ushering in the age of organized crime and as a spin-off a great increase in drinking in that country and later on, all those wonderful gangster films. The same year, the partition of Ireland took place bringing more conflict and this time on a very long-term basis.

1930 – 1939

The 1930s should have been better than the 1920s but they were not. Pluto remained in Cancer until 1937, Neptune remained in Virgo throughout the decade, Uranus entered Taurus in 1934 and Saturn moved from Capricorn through Aquarius, Pisces then back and forth between Aries and Pisces, ending the decade in Taurus.

The stars and the decade

Neptune's voyage through Virgo did help in the field of advances in medicine and in public health. Pluto continued to make life hard for men and then by extension for families, while in the 'motherhood' sign of Cancer. While Saturn was in the governmental signs of Capricorn and Aquarius, democracy ceased to exist anywhere in the world. In the UK a coalition government was in power for most of the decade while in the USA, Franklin Delano Roosevelt ruled as a kind of benign emperor for almost three terms of office, temporarily dismantling much of that country's democratic machinery while he did so. Governments in Russia, Germany, Italy, Spain and Japan moved to dictatorships or dictatorial types of government with all the resultant tyranny, while France, Britain and even the USA floundered for much of the time. China was ruled by warring factions. However, there was an upsurge of popular entertainment at this time, especially through the mediums of film, music and radio probably due to the advent of adventurous, inventive Uranus into the music and entertainment sign of Taurus in 1934.

1940 – 1949

War years once again. Pluto remained in the 'paternal' sign of Leo throughout this decade, bringing tyranny and control of the masses in all the developed countries and also much of the Third World. Neptune entered Libra in 1942, Uranus moved from Taurus to Gemini in 1941, then to Cancer in 1948. Saturn began the decade in Taurus, moved to Gemini, Cancer, Leo and finally Virgo during this decade. The 'home and country' signs of Cancer and Leo were once more thrust into the limelight in a war context. Neptune is not a particularly warlike planet and Libra is normally a peaceable sign but Libra does rule open enemies as well as peace and harmony.

The stars and the decade

To continue looking for the moment at the planet Neptune, astrologers don't take its dangerous side seriously enough. Neptune can use the sea in a particularly destructive manner when it wants to with tidal waves, disasters at sea and so on, so it is interesting to note that the war in the West was almost lost for the allies at sea due to the success of the German U-boats. Hitler gambled on a quick end to the war in the east and shut his mind to Napoleon's experience of the Russian winter. Saturn through Cancer and Leo, followed by the inventive sign of Uranus entering Cancer at the end of the decade almost brought home, family, tradition and the world itself to an end with the explosions of the first atomic bombs.

However, towards the end of this decade, it became clear that democracy, the rights of ordinary people and a better lifestyle for everybody were a better answer than trying to find 'lebensraum' by pinching one's neighbour's land and enslaving its population. Saturn's entry into Virgo brought great advances in medicine and the plagues and diseases of the past began to diminish throughout the world. Pluto in Leo transformed the power structures of every country and brought such ideas as universal education, better housing and social security systems - at least in the developed world.

1950 – 1959

Pluto still dipped in and out of Leo until it finally left for Virgo in 1957. Neptune finally left Libra for Scorpio in 1955, Uranus sat on that dangerous and warlike cusp of Cancer and Leo, while Saturn moved swiftly through Virgo, Libra, Scorpio, Sagittarius and then into Capricorn.

The stars and the decade

The confrontations between dictators and between dictatorships and democracy continued during this time with the emphasis shifting to the conflict between communism and capitalism. The Korean war started the decade and the communist take-over in China ended it. Military alertness was reflected in the UK by the two years of national service that young men were obliged to perform throughout the decade. Rationing, shortages of food, fuel and consumer goods remained in place for half the decade, but by the end of it, the world was becoming a very different place. With American money, Germany and Japan were slowly rebuilt, communism did at least bring a measure of stability in China and the Soviet Union, although its pervasive power brought fear and peculiar witch hunts in the United States. In Europe and the USA the lives of ordinary people improved beyond belief.

Pluto in Virgo brought plenty of work for the masses and for ordinary people, poverty began to recede for the first time in history. Better homes, labour-saving devices and the vast amount of popular entertainment in the cinema, the arts, popular music and television at long last brought fun into the lives of most ordinary folk. In Britain and the Commonwealth, in June 1953, the coronation of the new Queen ushered in a far more optimistic age while her Empire dissolved around her.

AQUARIUS

1960 – 1969

This is the decade that today's middle-aged folk look back on with fond memories, yet it was not always as safe as we like to think. Pluto remained in Virgo throughout the decade bringing work and better health to many people. Neptune remained in Scorpio throughout this time, while Uranus traversed back and forth between Leo and Virgo, then from Virgo to Libra, ending the decade in Libra. Saturn hovered around the cusp of Taurus and Gemini until the middle of the decade and then on through Gemini and Cancer, spending time around the Cancer/Leo cusp and then on through Leo to rest once again on the Leo/Virgo cusp.

The stars and the decade

The Cancer/Leo threats of atomic war were very real in the early 1960s, with the Cuban missile crisis bringing America and the Soviet Union to the point of war. The Berlin wall went up. President Kennedy's assassination in November 1963 shocked the world and the atmosphere of secrets, spies and mistrust abounded in Europe, the USA and in the Soviet Union. One of the better manifestations of this time of cold war, CIA dirty tricks and spies was the plethora of wonderful spy films and television programmes of the early 60s. Another was the sheer fun of the Profumo affair!

The late 1960s brought the start of a very different atmosphere. The Vietnam War began to be challenged by the teenagers whose job it was to die in it and the might of America was severely challenged by these tiny Vietcong soldiers in black pyjamas and sandals. The wave of materialism of the 1950s was less attractive to the flower-power generation of the late 60s. The revolutionary planet Uranus in balanced Libra brought the protest movement into being and an eventual end to racial segregation in the USA. Equality between the sexes was beginning to be considered. The troubles of Northern Ireland began at the end of this decade.

In 1969, Neil Armstrong stepped out onto the surface of the Moon, thereby marking the start of a very different age, the New Age, the Age of Aquarius.

1970 – 1979

Pluto began the decade around the Virgo/Libra cusp, settling in Libra in 1972 and remaining there for the rest of the decade. Neptune started the decade by moving back and forth between Scorpio and Sagittarius and residing in Sagittarius for the rest of the decade. Uranus hovered between Libra and Scorpio until 1975 and then travelled through Scorpio until the end of the decade while Saturn moved from Taurus to Gemini, then hung around the Cancer/Leo cusp and finally moved into Virgo.

The stars and the decade

The planets in or around that dangerous Cancer/Leo cusp and the continuing Libran emphasis brought more danger from total war as America struggled with Vietnam and the cold war. However, the influence of Virgo brought work, an easier life and more hope than ever to ordinary people in the First World. Uranus in Libra brought different kinds of love partnerships into public eye as fewer people bothered to marry. Divorce became easier and homosexuality became legal. With Uranus opening the doors to secretive Scorpio, spies such as Burgess, Maclean, Philby, Lonsdale and Penkowski began to come in from the cold. President Nixon was nicely caught out at Watergate, ushering in a time of more openness in governments everywhere.

If you are reading this book, you may be doing so because you are keen to know about yourself and your sign, but you are likely to be quite interested in astrology and perhaps in other esoteric techniques. You can thank the atmosphere of the 1970s for the openness and the lack of fear and superstition which these subjects now enjoy. The first festival of Mind, Body and Spirit took place in 1976 and the British Astrological and Psychic Society was launched in the same year, both of these events being part of the increasing interest in personal awareness and alternative lifestyles.

Neptune in Scorpio brought fuel crises and Saturn through Cancer and Leo brought much of the repression of women to an end, with some emancipation from tax and social anomalies. Tea bags and instant coffee allowed men for the first time to cope with the terrible hardship of making a cuppa!

1980 - 1989

Late in 1983, Pluto popped into the sign of Scorpio, popped out again and re-entered it in 1984. Astrologers of the 60s and 70s feared this planetary situation in case it brought the ultimate Plutonic destruction with it. Instead of this, the Soviet Union and South Africa freed themselves from tyranny and the Berlin Wall came down. The main legacy of Pluto in Scorpio is the Scorpionic association of danger through sex, hence the rise of AIDS. Neptune began the decade in Sagittarius then it travelled back and forth over the Sagittarius/Capricorn cusp, ending the decade in Capricorn. Uranus moved from Scorpio, back and forth over the Scorpio/Sagittarius cusp, then through Sagittarius, ending the decade in Capricorn. Saturn began the decade in Virgo, then hovered around the Virgo/Libra cusp, through Libra, Scorpio and Sagittarius, resting along the Sagittarius/Capricorn cusp, ending the decade in Capricorn.

The stars and the decade

The movement of planets through the dynastic sign of Sagittarius brought doubt and uncertainty to Britain's royal family, while the planets in authoritative Capricorn brought strong government to the UK in the form of Margaret Thatcher. Ordinary people began to seriously question the *status quo* and to attempt to change it. Even in the hidden empire of China, modernization and change began to creep in. Britain went to war again by sending the gunboats to the Falkland Islands to fight off a truly old-fashioned takeover bid by the daft Argentinean dictator, General Galtieri.

Saturn is an earth planet, Neptune rules the sea, while Uranus is associated with the air. None of these planets was in their own element and this may have had something to do with the increasing number of natural and man-made disasters that disrupted the surface of the earth during this decade. The first space shuttle flight took place in 1981 and the remainder of the decade reflected many people's interest in extra-terrestrial life in the form of films and television programmes. ET went home. Black rap music and the casual use of drugs became a normal part of the youth scene. Maybe the movement of escapist Neptune through the 'outer space' sign of Sagittarius had something to do with this.

1990 – 1999

Pluto began the decade in Scorpio, moving in and out of Sagittarius until 1995 remaining there for the rest of the decade. Neptune began the decade in Capricorn, travelling back and forth over the cusp of Aquarius, ending the decade in Aquarius, Uranus moved in and out of Aquarius, remaining there from 1996 onwards. Saturn travelled from Capricorn, through Aquarius, Pisces (and back again), then on through Pisces, Aries, in and out of Taurus, finally ending the decade in Taurus.

The stars and the decade

The Aquarian emphasis has brought advances in science and technology and a time when computers are common even in the depths of darkest Africa. The logic and fairness of Aquarius does seem to have affected many of the peoples of the earth. Pluto in the open sign of Sagittarius brought much governmental secrecy to an end, it will also transform the traditional dynasties of many countries before it leaves them for good. The aftermath of the dreadful and tragic death of Princess Diana in 1997 put a rocket under the creaking 19th-century habits of British royalty.

The final decade began with yet another war – this time the Gulf War – which sent a serious signal to all those who fancy trying their hand at international bullying or the 19th-century tactics of pinching your neighbour's land and resources. Uranus's last fling in Capricorn tore up the earth with volcanoes and earthquakes, and its stay in Aquarius seems to be keeping this pattern going. Saturn in Pisces, opposite the 'health' sign of Virgo is happily bringing new killer viruses into being and encouraging old ones to build up resistance to antibiotics. The bubonic plague is alive and well in tropical countries along with plenty of other plagues that either are, or are becoming resistant to modern medicines. Oddly enough the planetary line-up in 1997 was similar to that of the time of the great plague of London in 1665!

Films, the arts, architecture all showed signs of beginning an exciting period of revolution in 1998. Life became more electronic and computer-based for the younger generation while in the old world, the vast army of the elderly began to struggle with a far less certain world of old-age poverty and strange and frightening innovations. Keeping up to date and learning to adapt is the only way to survive now, even for the old folks.

It is interesting to note that the first event of importance to shock Europe in this century was the morganatic marriage of Franz Ferdinand, the heir to the massively powerful Austro-Hungarian throne. This took place in the summer of 1900. The unpopularity of this controlling and repressive empire fell on its head in Sarajevo on the 28th of July 1914. This mighty empire is now almost forgotten, but its death throes are still being played out in and around Sarajevo today - which only goes to show how long it can take for anything to be settled.

Technically the twentieth century only ends at the beginning of the year 2001 but most of us will be celebrating the end of the century and the end of the millennium and the end of the last day of 1999 - that is if we are all here of course! A famous prediction of global disaster comes from the writings of the French writer, doctor and astrologer Nostradamus (1503–66):

- The year 1999, seventh month,
- From the sky will come a great King of Terror:
- To bring back to life the great King of the Mongols,
- Before and after Mars reigns.
  (Quatrain X:72 from the *Centuries*)

Jonathan has worked out that with the adjustments of the calendar from the time of Nostradamus, the date of the predicted disaster will be the 11th of August 1999. As it happens there will be a total eclipse of the Sun at ten past eleven on that day at 18 degrees of Leo. We have already seen how the signs of Cancer, Leo and Libra seem to be the ones that are most clearly associated with war and this reference to 'Mars reigning' is the fact that Mars is the god of war. Therefore, the prediction suggests that an Oriental king will wage a war from the sky that brings terror to the world. Some people have suggested that this event would bring about the end of the world but that is not what the prediction actually says. A look back over the 1900s has proved this whole century to be one of terror from the skies but it would be awful to think that there would be yet another war, this time emanating from Mongolia. Terrible but not altogether impossible to imagine I guess. Well, let us hope that we are all here for us to write and for you to enjoy the next set of zodiac books for the turn of the millennium and beyond.

2000 onwards: a very brief look forward

The scientific exploration and eventual colonization of space is on the way now. Scorpio rules fossil fuels and there will be no major planets passing through this sign for quite a while so alternative fuel sources will have to be sought. Maybe it will be the entry of Uranus into the pioneering sign of Aries in January 2012 that will make a start on this. The unusual line up of the 'ancient seven' planets of Sun, Moon, Mercury, Venus, Mars and Saturn in Taurus on the 5th of May 2000 will be interesting. Taurus represents such matters as land, farming, building, cooking, flowers, the sensual beauty of music, dancing and the arts. Jonathan and Sasha will work out the astrological possibilities for the future in depth and put out ideas together for you in a future book.

The Essential Aquarius

YOUR RULING PLANET Your ruling body is Uranus. This planet behaves very differently from all the others in the Solar system, and therefore it represents unpredictable behaviour and eccentricity. Before the discovery of Uranus, Saturn was considered to be the ruler of Aquarius.

YOUR SYMBOL The water carrier is your symbol. This confuses beginners in astrology because Aquarius is actually an air sign. The water carrier represents a reservoir of knowledge which is hidden in the water. Other aspects of this deep symbol include a cloud of water, carried through the air. This is a frightening symbol for people of the post-World War II generation, because it carries images of nuclear fallout. Uranium is, of course, associated with Aquarius.

PARTS OF THE BODY The ankles and circulation to the extremities. Also breathing.

YOUR GOOD BITS You are friendly, independent and talented and you have an excellent mind.

YOUR BAD BITS It is hard for you to get in touch with your own emotions. You rebel against authority and you can be eccentric and 'difficult' at times.

YOUR WEAKNESSES Your ability to argue logically (and endlessly).

YOUR BEST DAY Saturday. Before the planet Uranus was discovered, your ruling planet was Saturn and Saturday is Saturn's day.

YOUR WORST DAY Monday. This is the Moon's day and the Moon is a watery, emotional planet that is very different in character from the logical Uranus.

YOUR COLOURS Neon colours, electric blue, indigo.

CITIES Salisbury, Hamburg, Bremen, Moscow, Toronto.

COUNTRIES Russia, Sweden, Ethiopia.

HOLIDAYS You like interesting places that offer good quality food and accommodation. You would probably enjoy a visit to the Kennedy Space Centre in Florida. Aquarians cannot be categorized but, generally speaking, you are not great travellers.

YOUR FAVOURITE CAR Something with a good engine and plenty of power. You may enjoy a digital dashboard with a computerized display showing inside and outside temperatures, a moving map, a tracking device for local speed traps or a wonderful sound system. This space-age machine will be kept in pristine condition, or it will be utterly filthy.

YOUR FAVOURITE MEAL OUT You may be a vegetarian or a 'funny' eater. If not, you enjoy experimenting with ethnic cuisine such as Chinese, Jewish, Italian or any kind of specialized food.

YOUR FAVOURITE DRINK You enjoy talking over a drink and a meal with friends, so plenty of red wine, beer, lager or any other type of social drink is acceptable.

YOUR HERBS Your sign is probably more attuned to spices like cumin rather than herbs, but the fennel plant is also associated with Aquarius.

YOUR TREE The willow.

YOUR FLOWERS Orchids, absinthe, buttercup.

YOUR ANIMALS Cat, hare, mouse.

YOUR METAL These days uranium is considered to be the metal for your sign, but lead was the old metal associated with Saturn, the old ruler of Aquarius. Platinum is also considered to be an Aquarian metal.

YOUR GEMS There are two gems associated with your sign. One is lapis lazuli and the other is amethyst. Many Aquarians enjoy buying crystals such as amethyst for meditation or healing purposes.

MODE OF DRESS You may choose clothes that are stylish, casual or totally individual and quite eccentric. You hate fussy clothes.

YOUR CAREERS Teacher, designer, computer expert, astrologer, counsellor, healer or anything else that is unusual.

YOUR FRIENDS You need plenty of friends and they must be clever, kind-hearted, interesting and humorous.

YOUR ENEMIES Over-emotional people who are clingy and want to drain you.

YOUR FAVOURITE GIFT You may be eccentric, but you do appreciate a touch of luxury. Therefore a good-quality gift that reflects your special interest would suit you. You may collect china animals or Japanese tea sets, so an addition to your collection would be nice. Another idea would be a reading with an astrologer. Otherwise, bookshelves and plenty of books to put on them, electronic gadgets and anything to do with computers.

YOUR IDEAL HOME Aquarians are so peculiar that it is hard to say how you would choose to live. Some of you like a home full of animals, children, noise and mess, whereas others need a sparse, cool-looking home with lots of space. Some love soft, feminine colours while others would enjoy living with stark, modern black-and-white furnishings. Many of you love the idea of living in an old castle or some other ancient pile that is filled with antiques and interesting junk.

YOUR FAVOURITE BOOKS Owning books is as important to you as reading them and you encourage your family to do the same. You love to be surrounded by books, newspapers, magazines, pamphlets and bits of paper with writing on them. To do you justice however, you do try to read everything within your reach and will even read the advertising on a packet of loo-paper rather than have nothing for your eyes to wander over. Many Aquarians enjoy science fiction and books about interesting and outlandish things such as UFOs.

YOUR FAVOURITE MUSIC This could be anything from classical to rock music, but you don't much care for background 'muzak'. Some of you love jazz or clever synthesizer music, while others are keen on meditation music of the kind that has dolphins and groaning whales doing a singalong!

YOUR GAMES AND SPORTS Word games such as scrabble and also

chess. You probably don't enjoy team games, but golf may appeal or anything you can do alone, such as fishing. Many Aquarians like tap or ballroom dancing. To be honest, you prefer attending interesting seminars (especially about astrology) and committee meetings to any kind of game or sport.

YOUR PAST AND FUTURE LIVES There are many theories about past lives and even some about future ones, but we suggest that your immediate past life was ruled by the sign previous to Aquarius and that your future life will be governed by the sign that follows Aquarius. Therefore you were Capricorn in your previous life and will be Pisces in the next. If you want to know all about either of these signs, zip straight out to the shops and buy our books on them!

YOUR LUCKY NUMBER Your lucky number is 2. To find your lucky number on a raffle ticket or something similar, first add the number together. For example, if one of your lottery numbers is 28, add 2 + 8 to make 10; then add 1 + 0, to give the root number of 1. The number 316 on a raffle ticket works in the same way. Add 3 + 1 + 6 to make 10: then add 1 + 0, making 1. As your lucky number is anything that adds up to 2, numbers such as 11, 974 or 281 would work. A selection of lottery numbers should include some of the following: 2, 11, 20, 29, 38 and 47.

AQUARIUS

Your Sun Sign

Your Sun Sign is determined by your date of birth.
Thus anyone born between 21st March and 20th April is Aries and so
on through the calendar. Your Rising Sign (see page 36)
is determined by the day and time of your birth.

AQUARIUS

RULED BY URANUS AND SATURN
21st January to 19th February

Yours is a masculine, air sign whose symbol is the water carrier. This adds intellectualism and inventiveness to your personality.

You are a stubborn and decisive character who feels comfortable in the realm of ideas, but you may find personal relationships or family life a bit difficult to deal with. Aquarians are different from just about everyone else, including all the other Aquarians and this makes you hard to categorize. You are extremely independent and your mode of thinking is totally individual; you prefer to be more of a lone wolf rather than a sheep following others. You also allow others to have their space and to do their own thing, as long as it does not impose on your own sense of freedom. You enjoy living in a relationship and you may even choose a conventional type of marriage but, if this doesn't work out, you have the ability to put the past behind you and move on to other things. You can live alone for periods of time but you don't enjoy it much, as you are happier as part of a team. You can be strangely blind in personal relationships. Sometimes this means that you simply don't notice when a family member is unhappy. Another problem that this blindness can bring is that you can find yourself living with someone who has a really impossible nature, because somehow you missed the danger signs before becoming totally committed. By far the most comfortable relationship for you is that of friendship. You have an open, humorous, non-hostile outer manner which draws people to you, and you really enjoy the company of your friends. You are the first to help someone out when they are in trouble. Some of you enjoy group activities, such as belonging to social clubs and political organizations, while other Aquarians avoid such things like the plague. Participant or not, you will always have plenty of good friends around you. You can be a very successful parent because you don't seek to smother your children or to treat them like idiots. You value education highly and see it as the road to success, wealth and independence and, therefore, you will do all you can to help your children get on. You never actually stop learning throughout life, so you would understand if your partner wanted to stop work to study for a while.

Aquarians can be found in any number of careers but anything that allows you to communicate with others is bound to appeal to you. You are drawn to work in the public sector and in technical jobs of one kind or another, with computers being a really hot favourite. You may choose to teach or write for a living. A friend of ours told us that she once worked in a firm that was being refurbished and every one of the eleven self-employed builders working on the job was an Aquarian! You have the most original mind of the zodiac and you may spend your life solving problems or inventing new and original methods. One thing for sure is that you won't spend much time slumped in front of a television.

You have a broad mind and an easy-going attitude to other people's eccentricities, but you baulk at having your own eccentricities challenged. The sign of Aquarius is associated with astrology and there are indeed many Aquarian astrologers. Other interests can include green issues, Egyptology, magic, the Tarot and alternative health and healing. However, you form your own philosophy of life rather early and you don't change your opinions easily.

All the Other Sun Signs

ARIES
21st March to 20th April

Ariens can get anything they want off the ground, but they may land back down again with a bump. Quick to think and to act, Ariens are often intelligent and have little patience with fools. This includes anyone who is slower than themselves.

They are not the tidiest of people and they are impatient with details, except when engaged upon their special subject; then Ariens can fiddle around for hours. They are willing to make huge financial sacrifices for their families and they can put up with relatives living with them as long as this leaves them free to do their own thing. Aries women are decisive and competitive at work but many are disinterested in homemaking. They might consider giving up a relationship if it interfered with their ambitions. Highly sexed and experimental, they are faithful while in love but, if love begins to fade, they start to look around. Ariens may tell themselves that they are only looking for amusement, but they may end up in a fulfilling relationship with someone else's partner. This kind of situation offers the continuity and emotional support which they need with no danger of boredom or entrapment.

Their faults are those of impatience and impetuosity, coupled with a hot temper. They can pick a furious row with a supposed adversary, tear him or her to pieces then walk away from the situation five minutes later, forgetting all about it. Unfortunately, the poor victim can't always shake off the effects of the row in quite the same way. However, Arien cheerfulness, spontaneous generosity and kindness make them the greatest friends to have.

TAURUS
21st April to 21st May

These people are practical and persevering. Taureans are solid and reliable, regular in habits, sometimes a bit wet behind the ears and stubborn as mules. Their love of money and the comfort it can bring may make them very materialistic in outlook. They are most suited to a practical career which brings with it few surprises and plenty of money. However, they have a strong artistic streak which can be expressed in work, hobbies and interests.

Some Taureans are quick and clever, highly amusing and quite outrageous in appearance, but underneath this crazy exterior is a background of true talent and very hard work. This type may be a touch arrogant. Other Taureans hate to be rushed or hassled, preferring to work quietly and thoroughly at their own pace. They take relationships very seriously and make safe and reliable partners. They may keep their worries to themselves but they are not usually liars or sexually untrustworthy.

Being so very sensual as well as patient, these people make excellent lovers. Their biggest downfall comes later in life when they have a tendency to plonk themselves down in front of the television night after night, tuning out the rest of the world. Another problem with some Taureans is their 'pet hate', which they'll harp on about at any given opportunity. Their virtues are common sense, loyalty, responsibility and a pleasant, non-hostile approach to others. Taureans are much brighter than anyone gives them credit, and it is hard to beat them in an argument because they usually know what they are talking about. If a Taurean is on your side, they make wonderful friends and comfortable and capable colleagues.

GEMINI
22nd May to 21st June

Geminis are often accused of being short on intellect and unable to stick to anyone or anything for long. In a nutshell, great fun at a party but totally unreliable. This is unfair: nobody works harder, is more reliable or capable than Geminis when they put their mind to a task, especially if there is a chance of making large sums of money! Unfortunately, they have a low boredom threshold and they can drift away from something or someone when it no longer interests them. They like to be busy, with plenty of variety in their lives and the opportunity to communicate with others. Their forte lies in the communications industry where they shamelessly pinch ideas and improve on them. Many Geminis are highly ambitious people who won't allow anything or anyone to stand in their way.

They are surprisingly constant in relationships, often marrying for life but, if it doesn't work out, they will walk out and put the experience behind them. Geminis need relationships and if one fails, they will soon start looking for the next. Faithfulness is another story, however, because the famous Gemini curiosity can lead to any number of adventures. Geminis educate their children well while neglecting to see whether they have a clean shirt. The house is full of books, videos, televisions, CDs, newspapers and magazines and there is a phone in every room as well as in the car, the loo and the Gemini lady's handbag.

CANCER
22nd June to 23rd July

Cancerians look for security on the one hand and adventure and novelty on the other. They are popular because they really listen to what others are saying. Their own voices are attractive too. They are naturals for sales work and in any kind of advisory capacity. Where their own problems are concerned, they can disappear inside themselves and brood, which makes it hard for others to understand them. Cancerians spend a good deal of time worrying about their families and, even more so, about money. They appear soft but are very hard to influence.

Many Cancerians are small traders and many more work in teaching or the caring professions. They have a feel for history, perhaps collecting historical mementoes, and their memories are excellent. They need to have a home but they love to travel away from it, being happy in the knowledge that it is there waiting for them to come back to. There are a few Cancerians who seem to drift through life and expect other members of their family to keep them.

AQUARIUS

Romantically, they prefer to be settled and they fear being alone. A marriage would need to be really bad before they consider leaving, and if they do, they soon look for a new partner. These people can be scoundrels in business because they hate parting with money once they have their hands on it. However, their charm and intelligence usually manage to get them out of trouble.

LEO
24th July to 23rd August

Leos can be marvellous company or a complete pain in the neck. Under normal circumstances, they are warm-hearted, generous, sociable and popular but they can be very moody and irritable when under pressure or under the weather. Leos put their heart and soul into whatever they are doing and they can work like demons for a while. However, they cannot keep up the pace for long and they need to get away, zonk out on the sofa and take frequent holidays. These people always appear confident and they look like true winners, but their confidence can suddenly evaporate, leaving them unsure and unhappy with their efforts. They are extremely sensitive to hurt and they cannot take ridicule or even very much teasing.

Leos are proud. They have very high standards in all that they do and most have great integrity and honesty, but there are some who are complete and utter crooks. These people can stand on their dignity and be very snobbish. Their arrogance can become insufferable and they can take their powers of leadership into the realms of bossiness. They are convinced that they should be in charge and they can be very obstinate. Some Leos love the status and lifestyle which proclaims their successes. Many work in glamour professions such as the airline and entertainment industries. Others spend their day communing with computers and other high-tech gadgetry. In loving relationships, they are loyal but only while the magic lasts. If boredom sets in, they often start looking around for fresh fields. They are the most generous and loving of people and they need to play affectionately. Leos are kind, charming and they live life to the full.

VIRGO
24th August to 23rd September

Virgos are highly intelligent, interested in everything and everyone and happy to be busy with many jobs and hobbies. Many have some kind of specialized knowledge and most are good with their hands, but their nit-picking ways can infuriate colleagues. They find it hard to discuss their innermost feelings and this can make them hard to understand. In many ways, they are happier doing something practical than dealing with relationships. Virgos can also overdo the self-sacrificial bit and make themselves martyrs to other people's impractical lifestyles. They are willing to fit in with whatever is going on and can adjust to most things, but they mustn't neglect their own needs.

Although excellent communicators and wonderfully witty conversationalists, Virgos prefer to express their deepest feelings by actions rather than words. Most avoid touching all but very close friends and family members and many find lovey-dovey behaviour embarrassing. They can be very highly sexed and may use this as a way of expressing love. Virgos are criticized a good deal as children and are often made to feel unwelcome in their childhood homes. In turn, they become very critical of others and they can use this in order to wound.

Many Virgos overcome inhibitions by taking up acting, music, cookery or sports. Acting is particularly common to this sign because it allows them to put aside their fears and take on the mantle of someone quite different. They are shy and slow to make friends but when they do accept someone, they are the loyalest, gentlest and kindest of companions. They are great company and have a wonderful sense of humour.

LIBRA
24th September to 23rd October

Librans have a deceptive appearance, looking soft but being tough and quite selfish underneath. Astrological tradition tells us that this sign is dedicated to marriage, but a high proportion of them prefer to remain single, particularly when a difficult relationship comes to an end. These people are great to tell secrets to because they never listen to anything properly and promptly forget whatever is said. The confusion between their desire to co-operate with others and the need for self-expression is even more evident when at work. The best job is one where they are a part of an organization but able to take responsibility and make their own decisions.

While some Librans are shy and lacking in confidence, others are strong and determined with definite leadership qualities. All need to find a job that entails dealing with others and which does not wear out their delicate nerves. All Librans are charming, sophisticated and diplomatic, but can be confusing for others. All have a strong sense of justice and fair play but most haven't the strength to take on a determinedly lame duck. They project an image which is attractive, chosen to represent their sense of status and refinement. Being inclined to experiment sexually, they are not the most faithful of partners and even goody-goody Librans are terrible flirts.

SCORPIO
24th October to 22nd November

Reliable, resourceful and enduring, Scorpios seem to be the strong men and women of the zodiac. But are they really? They can be nasty at times, dishing out what they see as the truth, no matter how unwelcome. Their own feelings are sensitive and they are easily hurt, but they won't show any hurt or weakness in themselves to others. When they are very low or unhappy, this turns inwards, attacking their immune systems and making them ill. However, they have great resilience and they bounce back time and again from the most awful ailments.

Nobody needs to love and be loved more than a Scorpio, but their partners must stand up to them because they will give anyone they don't respect a very hard time indeed. They are the most loyal and honest of companions, both in personal relationships and at work. One reason for this is their hatred of change or uncertainty. Scorpios enjoy being the power behind the throne with someone else occupying the hot seat. This way, they can quietly manipulate everyone, set one against another and get exactly what they want from the situation.

Scorpios' voices are their best feature, often low, well-modulated and cultured and these wonderful voices are used to the full in pleasant persuasion. These people are neither as highly sexed nor as difficult as most astrology books make out, but they do have their passions (even if these are not always for sex itself) and they like to be thought of as sexy. They love to shock and to appear slightly dangerous, but they also make kind-hearted and loyal friends, superb hosts and gentle people who are often very fond of animals. Great people when they are not being cruel, stingy or devious!

SAGITTARIUS
23rd November to 21st December

Sagittarians are great company because they are interested in everything and everyone. Broad-minded and lacking in prejudice, they are fascinated by even the strangest of people. With their optimism and humour, they are often the life and soul of the party, while they are in a good mood. They can become quite down-hearted, crabby and awkward on occasion, but not usually for long. They can be hurtful to others because they cannot resist speaking what they see as the truth, even if it causes embarrassment. However, their tactlessness is usually innocent and they have no desire to hurt.

Sagittarians need an unconventional lifestyle, preferably one which allows them to travel. They cannot be cooped up in a cramped environment and they need to meet new people and to explore a variety of ideas during their day's work. Money is not their god and they will work for a pittance if they feel inspired by the task. Their values are spiritual rather than material. Many are attracted to the spiritual side of life and may be interested in the Church, philosophy, astrology and other New Age subjects. Higher education and legal matters attract them because these subjects expand and explore intellectual boundaries. Long-lived relationships may not appeal because they need to feel free and unfettered, but they can do well with a self-sufficient and independent partner. Despite all this intellectualism and need for freedom, Sagittarians have a deep need to be cuddled and touched and they need to be supported emotionally.

CAPRICORN
22nd December to 20th January

Capricorns are patient, realistic and responsible and they take life seriously. They need security but they may find this difficult to achieve. Many live on a treadmill of work, simply to pay the bills and feed the kids. They will never shun family responsibilities, even caring for distant relatives if this becomes necessary. However, they can play the martyr while doing so. These people hate coarseness, they are easily embarrassed and they hate to annoy anyone. Capricorns believe fervently in keeping the peace in their families. This doesn't mean that they cannot stand up for themselves, indeed they know how to get their own way and they won't be bullied. They are adept at using charm to get around prickly people.

Capricorns are ambitious, hard-working, patient and status-conscious and they will work their way steadily towards the top in any organization. If they run their own businesses, they need a partner with more pizzazz to deal with sales and marketing for them while they keep an eye on the books. Their nit-picking habits can infuriate others and some have a tendency to 'know best' and not to listen. These people work at their hobbies with the same kind of dedication that they put into everything else. They are faithful and reliable in relationships and it takes a great deal to make them stray. If a relationship breaks up, they take a long time to get over it. They may marry very early or delay it until middle age when they are less shy. As an earth sign, Capricorns are highly sexed but they need to be in a relationship where they can relax and gain confidence. Their best attribute is their genuine kindness and their wonderfully dry, witty sense of humour.

PISCES
20th February to 20th March

This idealistic, dreamy, kind and impractical sign needs a lot of understanding. They have a fractured personality which has so many sides and so many moods that they probably don't even understand themselves. Nobody is more kind, thoughtful and caring, but they have a tendency to drift away from people and responsibilities. When the going gets rough, they get going! Being creative, clever and resourceful, these people can achieve a great deal and really reach the top, but few of them do. Some Pisceans have a self-destruct button which they press before reaching their goal. Others do achieve success and the motivating force behind this essentially spiritual and mystical sign is often money. Many Pisceans feel insecure, most suffer some experience of poverty at some time in their early lives and they grow into adulthood determined that they will never feel that kind of uncertainty again.

Pisceans are at home in any kind of creative or caring career. Many can be found in teaching, nursing and the arts. Some find life hard and are often unhappy; many have to make tremendous sacrifices on behalf of others. This may be a pattern which repeats itself from childhood, where the message is that the Piscean's needs always come last. These people can be stubborn, awkward, selfish and quite nasty when a friendship or relationship goes sour. This is because, despite their basically kind and gentle personality, there is a side which needs to be in charge of any relationship. Pisceans make extremely faithful partners as long as the romance doesn't evaporate and their partners treat them well. Problems occur if they are mistreated or rejected, if they become bored or restless or if their alcohol intake climbs over the danger level. The Piscean lover is a sexual fantasist, so in this sphere of life anything can happen!

You and Yours

What is it like to bring up an Arien child? What kind of father does a Libran make? How does it feel to grow up with a Sagittarian mother? Whatever your own sign is, how do you appear to your parents and how do you behave towards your children?

THE AQUARIAN FATHER

Some Aquarian men have no great desire to be fathers but they make a reasonable job of it when they have to. They cope best when their children are reasonable and intelligent but, if they are not, they tune out and ignore them. Some Aquarians will spend hours inventing games and toys for their children while all of them value education and try to push their children.

THE AQUARIAN MOTHER

Some of these mothers are too busy putting the world to rights to see what is going on in their own family. However, they are kind, reasonable and keen on education. They may be busy outside the house but they often take their children along with them. They are not fussy homemakers, and are happy to have all the neighbourhood kids in the house. They respect a child's dignity.

THE AQUARIAN CHILD

These children may be demanding when very young but they become much more reasonable when at school. They are easily bored and need outside interests. They have many friends and may spend more time in other people's homes than in their own. Very stubborn and determined, they make it quite clear from an early age that they intend to do things their own way. These children suffer from nerves.

THE ARIES FATHER

Arien men take the duties of fatherhood very seriously. They read to their children, take them on educational trips and expose them to art and music from an early age. They can push their children too hard or tyrannize the sensitive ones. The Aries father wants his children not only to have what he didn't have but also to be what he isn't. He respects those children who are high achievers and who can stand up to him.

THE ARIES MOTHER

Arien women love their children dearly and will make amazing sacrifices for them, but don't expect them to give up their jobs or their outside interests for motherhood. Competitive herself, this mother wants her children to be the best and she may push them too hard. However, she is kind-hearted, affectionate and not likely to over-discipline them. She treats her offspring as adults and is well loved in return.

THE ARIES CHILD

Arien children are hard to ignore. Lively, noisy and demanding, they try to enjoy every moment of their childhood. Despite this, they lack confidence and need reassurance. Often clever but lacking in self-discipline, they need to be made to attend school each day and to do their homework. Active and competitive, these children excel in sports, dancing or learning to play a pop music instrument.

THE TAURUS FATHER

This man cares deeply for his children and wants the best for them, but doesn't expect the impossible. He may lay the law down and he can be unsympathetic to the attitudes and interests of a new generation. He may frighten young children by shouting at them. Being a responsible parent, he offers a secure family base but he may find it hard to let them go when they want to leave.

THE TAURUS MOTHER

These women make good mothers due to their highly domesticated nature. Some are real earth mothers, baking bread and making wonderful toys and games for their children. Sane and sensible but not highly imaginative, they do best with a child who has ordinary needs and they get confused by those who are 'special' in any way. Taurus mothers are very loving but they use reasonable discipline when necessary.

THE TAURUS CHILD

Taurean children can be surprisingly demanding. Their loud voices and stubborn natures can be irritating. Plump, sturdy and strong, some are shy and retiring, while others can bully weaker children. Artistic, sensual and often musical, these children can lose themselves in creative or beautiful hobbies. They need to be encouraged to share and express love and also to avoid too many sweet foods.

THE GEMINI FATHER

Gemini fathers are fairly laid back in their approach and, while they cope well with fatherhood, they can become bored with home life and try to escape from their duties. Some are so absorbed with work that they hardly see their offspring. At home, Gemini fathers will provide books, educational toys and as much computer equipment as the child can use, and they enjoy a family game of tennis.

THE GEMINI MOTHER

These mothers can be very pushy because they see education as the road to success. They encourage a child to pursue any interest and will sacrifice time and money for this. They usually have a job outside the home and may rely on other people to do some child-minding for them. Their children cannot always count on coming home to a balanced meal, but they can talk to their mothers on any subject.

THE GEMINI CHILD

These children needs a lot of reassurance because they often feel like square pegs in round holes. They either do very well at school and incur the wrath of less able children, or they fail dismally and have to make it up later in life. They learn to read early and some have excellent mechanical ability while others excel at sports. They get bored very easily and they can be extremely irritating.

THE CANCER FATHER

A true family man who will happily embrace even stepchildren as if they were his own. Letting go of the family when they grow up is another matter. Cancerian sulks, moodiness and bouts of childishness can confuse or frighten some children, while his changeable attitude to money can make them unsure of what they should ask for. This father enjoys domesticity and child-rearing and he may be happy to swap roles.

THE CANCER MOTHER

Cancerian women are excellent home makers and cheerful and reasonable mothers, as long as they have a part-time job or an interest outside the house. They instinctively know when a child is unhappy and can deal with it in a manner which is both efficient and loving. These women have a reputation for clinging but most are quite realistic when the time comes for their brood to leave the nest.

THE CANCER CHILD

These children are shy, cautious and slow to grow up. They may achieve little at school, 'disappearing' behind louder and more demanding classmates. They can be worriers who complain about every ache and pain or suffer from imaginary fears. They may take on the mother's role in the family, dictating to their sisters and brothers at times. Gentle and loving but moody and secretive, they need a lot of love and encouragement.

THE LEO FATHER

These men can be wonderful fathers as long as they remember that children are not simply small and rather obstreperous adults. Leo fathers like to be involved with their children and encourage them to do well at school. They happily make sacrifices for their children and they truly want them to have the best, but they can be a bit too strict and they may demand too high a standard

THE LEO MOTHER

Leo mothers are very caring and responsible but they cannot be satisfied with a life of pure domesticity, and need to combine motherhood with a job. These mothers don't fuss about minor details. They're prepared to put up with a certain amount of noise and disruption, but they can be irritable and they may demand too much of their children.

THE LEO CHILD

These children know almost from the day they are born that they are special They are usually loved and wanted but they are also aware that a lot is expected from them. Leo children appear outgoing but they are surprisingly sensitive and easily hurt. They only seem to wake up to the need to study a day or so after they leave school, but they find a way to make a success of their lives.

THE VIRGO FATHER

These men may be embarrassed by open declarations of love and affection and find it hard to give cuddles and reassurance to small children. Yet they love their offspring dearly and will go to any lengths to see that they have the best possible education and outside activities. Virgoan men can become wrapped up in their work, forgetting to spend time relaxing and playing with their children

THE VIRGO MOTHER

Virgoan women try hard to be good mothers because they probably had a poor childhood themselves. They love their children very much and want the best for them but they may be fussy about unnecessary details, such as dirt on the kitchen floor or the state of the children's school books. If they can keep their tensions and longings away from their children, they can be the most kindly and loving parents.

THE VIRGO CHILD

Virgoan children are practical and capable and can do very well at school, but they are not always happy. They don't always fit in and they may have difficulty making friends. They may be shy, modest and sensitive and they can find it hard to live up to their own impossibly high standards. Virgo children don't need harsh discipline, they want approval and will usually respond perfectly well to reasoned argument.

THE LIBRA FATHER

Libran men mean well, but they may not actually perform that well. They have no great desire to be fathers but welcome their children when they come along. They may slide out of the more irksome tasks by having an absorbing job or a series of equally absorbing hobbies which keep them occupied outside the home. These men do better with older children because they can talk to them.

THE LIBRA MOTHER

Libran mothers are pleasant and easy-going but some of them are more interested in their looks, their furnishings and their friends than their children. Others are very loving and kind but a bit too soft, which results in their children disrespecting them or walking all over them in later life. These mothers enjoy talking to their children and encouraging them to succeed.

THE LIBRA CHILD

These children are charming and attractive and they have no difficulty in getting on with people. They make just enough effort to get through school and only do the household jobs they cannot dodge. They may drive their parents mad with their demands for the latest gadget or gimmick. However, their common sense, sense of humour and reasonable attitude makes harsh discipline unnecessary.

THE SCORPIO FATHER

These fathers can be really awful or absolutely wonderful, and there aren't any half-measures. Good Scorpio men provide love and security because they stick closely to their homes and families and are unlikely to do a disappearing act. Difficult ones can be loud and tyrannical. These proud men want their children to be the best.

THE SCORPIO MOTHER

These mothers are either wonderful or not really maternal at all, although they try to do their best. If they take to child-rearing, they encourage their offspring educationally and in their hobbies. These mothers have no time for whiny or miserable children but they respect outgoing, talented and courageous ones, and can cope with a handful.

THE SCORPIO CHILD

Scorpio children are competitive, self-centred and unwilling to co-operate with brothers, sisters, teachers or anyone else when in an awkward mood. They can be deeply unreadable, living in a world of their own and filled with all kinds of strange angry feelings. At other times, they can be delightfully caring companions. They love animals, sports, children's organizations and group activities.

THE SAGITTARIUS FATHER

Sagittarian fathers will give their children all the education they can stand. They happily provide books, equipment and take their offspring out to see anything interesting. They may not always be available to their offspring, but they make up for it by surprising their families with tickets for sporting events or by bringing home a pet for the children. These men are cheerful and childlike themselves.

THE SAGITTARIUS MOTHER

This mother is kind, easy-going and pleasant. She may be very ordinary with suburban standards or she may be unbelievably eccentric, forcing the family to take up strange diets and filling the house with weird and wonderful people. Some opt out of child-rearing by finding childminders while others take on other people's children and a host of animals in addition to their own.

THE SAGITTARIUS CHILD

Sagittarian children love animals and the outdoor life but they are just as interested in sitting around and watching the telly as the next child. These children have plenty of friends whom they rush out and visit at every opportunity. Happy and optimistic but highly independent, they cannot be pushed in any direction. Many leave home in late their teens in order to travel.

THE CAPRICORN FATHER

These are true family men who cope with housework and child-rearing but they are sometimes too involved in work to spend much time at home. Dutiful and caring, these men are unlikely to run off with a bimbo or to leave their family wanting. However, they can be stuffy or out of touch with the younger generation. They encourage their children to do well and to behave properly.

THE CAPRICORN MOTHER

Capricorn women make good mothers but they may be inclined to fuss. Being ambitious, they want their children to do well and they teach them to respect teachers, youth leaders and so on. These mothers usually find work outside the home in order to supplement the family income. They are very loving but they can be too keen on discipline and the careful management of pocket money.

THE CAPRICORN CHILD

Capricorn children are little adults from the day they are born. They don't need much discipline or encouragement to do well at school. Modest and well behaved, they are almost too good to be true. However, they suffer badly with their nerves and can be prone to ailments such as asthma. They need to be taught to let go, have fun and enjoy their childhood. Some are too selfish or ambitious to make friends.

THE PISCES FATHER

Piscean men fall into one of two categories. Some are kind and gentle, happy to take their children on outings and to introduce them to art, culture, music or sport. Others are disorganized and unpredictable. The kindly fathers don't always push their children. They encourage their kids to have friends and a pet or two.

THE PISCES MOTHER

Piscean mothers may be lax and absent-minded but they love their children and are usually loved in return. Many are too disorganized to run a perfect household so meals, laundry, etc. can be hit and miss, but their children prosper despite this, although many learn to reverse the mother/child roles. These mothers teach their offspring to appreciate animals and the environment.

THE PISCES CHILD

These sensitive children may find life difficult and they can get lost among stronger, more demanding brothers and sisters. They may drive their parents batty with their dreamy attitude and they can make a fuss over nothing. They need a secure and loving home with parents who shield them from harsh reality while encouraging them to develop their imaginative and psychic abilities.

Your Rising Sign

WHAT IS A RISING SIGN?
Your rising sign is the sign of the zodiac which was climbing up over the eastern horizon the moment you were born. This is not the same as your Sun sign; your Sun sign depends upon your date of birth, but your rising sign depends upon the time of day that you were born, combined with your date and place of birth.

The rising sign modifies your Sun sign character quite considerably, so when you have worked out which is your rising sign, read pages 39–40 to see how it modifies your Sun sign. Then take a deeper look by going back to 'All the Other Sun Signs' on page 21 and read the relevant Sun sign material there to discover more about your ascendant (rising sign) nature.

One final point is that the sign that is opposite your rising sign (or 'ascendant') is known as your 'descendant'. This shows what you want from other people, and it may give a clue as to your choice of friends, colleagues and lovers (see pages 41–3). So once you have found your rising sign and read the character interpretation, check out the character reading for your descendant to see what you are looking for in others.

How to Begin
Read through this section while following the example below. Even if you only have a vague idea of your birth time, you won't find this method difficult; just go for a rough time of birth and then read the Sun sign information for that sign to see if it fits your personality. If you seem to be more like the sign that comes before or after it, then it is likely that you were born a little earlier or later than your assumed time of birth. Don't forget to deduct an hour for summertime births.

1. Look at the illustration top right. You will notice that it has the time of day arranged around the outer circle. It looks a bit like a clock face, but it is different because it shows the whole 24-hour day in two-hour blocks.

2. Write the astrological symbol that represents the Sun (a circle with a dot in the middle) in the segment that corresponds to your time of birth. (If you were born during Daylight Saving or British Summer Time, deduct one hour from your birth time.) Our example shows someone who was born between 2 a.m. and 4 a.m.

3. Now write the name of your sign or the symbol for your sign on the line which is at the end of the block of time that your Sun falls into. Our example shows a person who was born between 2 a.m. and 4 a.m. under the sign of Pisces.

4. Either write in the names of the zodiac signs or use the symbols in their correct order (see the key below) around the chart in an anti-clockwise direction, starting from the line which is at the start of the block of time that your sun falls into.

5. The sign that appears on the left-hand side of the wheel at the 'Dawn' line is your rising sign, or ascendant. The example shows a person born with the Sun in Pisces and with Aquarius rising. Incidentally, the example chart also shows Leo, which falls on the 'Dusk' line, in the descendant. You will always find the ascendant sign on the 'Dawn' line and the descendant sign on the 'Dusk' line.

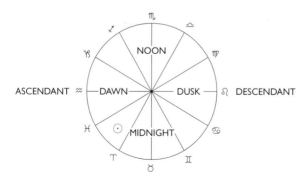

♈	Aries	♋	Cancer	♎	Libra	♑	Capricorn
♉	Taurus	♌	Leo	♏	Scorpio	♒	Aquarius
♊	Gemini	♍	Virgo	♐	Sagittarius	♓	Pisces

Here is another example for you to run through, just to make sure that you have grasped the idea correctly. This example is for a more awkward time of birth, being exactly on the line between two different blocks of time. This example is for a person with a Capricorn Sun sign who was born at 10 a.m.

1. The Sun is placed exactly on the 10 a.m. line.

2. The sign of Capricorn is placed on the 10 a.m. line.

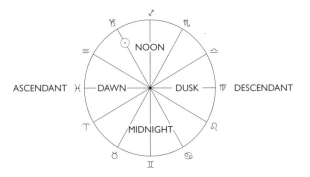

3. All the other signs are placed in astrological order (anti-clockwise) around the chart.

4. This person has the Sun in Capricorn and Pisces rising, and therefore with Virgo on the descendant.

Using the Rising Sign Finder

Please bear in mind that this method is approximate. If you want to be really sure of your rising sign, you should contact an astrologer. However, this system will work with reasonable accuracy wherever you were born. Check out the Sun and ascendant combination in the following pages. Once you've done so, if you're not quite sure you've got it right, you should also read the Sun sign character readings on pages 21–8 for the signs both before and after the rising sign you think is yours. Rising signs are such an obvious part of one's personality that one quick glance will show you which one belongs to you.

Can Your Rising Sign Tell You More about Your Future?

When it comes to tracking events, the rising sign is equal in importance to the Sun sign. So, if you want a more accurate forecast when reading newspapers or magazines, you should read the horoscope for your rising sign as well as your Sun sign. In the case of books such as this, you should really treat yourself to two: one to correspond with your rising sign, and another for your usual Sun sign, and read both each day!

How Your Rising Sign Modifies Your Sun Sign

AQUARIUS WITH ARIES RISING You are quite outgoing and you also have many friends and acquaintances. You enjoy working in large organizations or in a job where you can advise people.

AQUARIUS WITH TAURUS RISING This combination makes you very stubborn and determined, so you tend to choose a way of life and then stick to it. You are attracted to the arts and to literature.

AQUARIUS WITH GEMINI RISING Bright and breezy, intelligent and aware, you are great company and you have many friends. You are also quite ambitious, and you may travel in order to learn more about people.

AQUARIUS WITH CANCER RISING You may work in teaching, nursing, counselling or something similar. You are gentler and more family-minded than most Aquarians.

AQUARIUS WITH LEO RISING You are outgoing and full of fun. You need to enjoy life and you could also be very ambitious. Computer work may attract you and you would also make a very good astrologer.

AQUARIUS WITH VIRGO RISING Health and healing appeal to you, so you may take up aromatherapy or something similar. You work hard when you feel motivated.

AQUARIUS WITH LIBRA RISING You are intelligent, charming and good-looking, all of which help you achieve your ambitions. You are fond of children and you are also very creative and inventive.

AQUARIUS WITH SCORPIO RISING
You choose a way of life and then stick to it, even when it doesn't really work. You are stubborn and determined, but also helpful to those who are sad or in pain.

AQUARIUS WITH SAGITTARIUS RISING You could be a real oddball, being split between materialistic and spiritual goals. You love learning new things and your interests are wide-ranging and unusual.

AQUARIUS WITH CAPRICORN RISING This combination gives you executive ability and a go-getting nature. However, your confidence is not all that it seems and you need a steady partner to give you security.

AQUARIUS WITH AQUARIUS RISING This is Aquarius in its purest form; you are independent, eccentric and intelligent. You choose unusual jobs and many interesting friends. You would be quieter, gentler and quite psychic if born after dawn but tougher and more outgoing if born before.

AQUARIUS WITH PISCES RISING Mysticism and psychic matters appeal to you, partly because you are sensitive but also because you are attracted to mysticism. You could have been lonely when young.

Aquarius in Love

YOU NEED:

INDEPENDENCE You may have unusual ideas about how you want to live your life and the priorities that you choose. These must be respected and understood by your partner.

INTELLECT You cannot stand a dull or boring partner and there has to be more to any relationship than keeping up with the Jones's. You appreciate a partner who has a mind and interests of his/her own.

SOCIAL LIFE However much you love your family, you enjoy the company of other people and you appreciate a partner who is happy to welcome and entertain others, and who allows you to enjoy the company of family and friends.

YOU GIVE:

RESPECT You prefer to choose a partner whom you can respect and you do all you can to build their confidence rather than compete with or undermine them. You respect their ideas and you make room for their interests.

SEXUALITY Yours is a surprisingly sexy sign and you enjoy giving pleasure as well as receiving it. You express your deepest feelings through sex and are happier with a partner who appreciates this.

COMMUNICATION You love to chat about anything from politics or the state of the world to all those little day-to-day things. You don't keep the contents of your mind or the circumstances of your working life secret from your partner.

WHAT YOU CAN EXPECT FROM THE OTHER ZODIAC SIGNS:

ARIES *Truth, honesty, playfulness.* You can expect an open and honest relationship with no hidden agendas. Your Arien lover will be a bit childish at times, however.

TAURUS *Security, stability, comfort.* The Taurean will stand by you and try to improve your financial position. They will create a beautiful home and garden for you.

GEMINI *Stimulation, encouragement, variety.* This lover will never bore you; Geminis give encouragement and are always ready for an outing. They give emotional support too.

CANCER *Emotional security, companionship, help.* Cancerians will never leave you stranded at a party or alone when suffering from the flu. They always lend a hand when asked.

LEO *Affection, fun, loyalty.* Leo lovers are very steadfast and they would seek revenge on anyone who hurt a member of family. They enjoy romping and playing affectionate love games.

VIRGO *Clear thinking, kindness, humour.* Virgoans make intelligent and amusing partners. They can be critical but are never unkind. They take their responsibility towards you seriously.

LIBRA *Fairplay, sensuality, advice.* Librans will listen to your problems and give balanced and sensible advice. They are wonderfully inventive, and are affectionate lovers too.

SCORPIO *Truth, passion, loyalty.* Scorpios will take your interests as seriously as they do their own. They will stick by you when the going gets tough and they won't flannel you.

SAGITTARIUS *Honesty, fun, novelty.* Theses lovers will never bore you and they'll keep up with whatever pace you set. They seek the truth and they don't keep their feelings hidden.

CAPRICORN *Companionship, common sense,* laughter. Capricorns enjoy doing things together and they won't leave you in the lurch when the going gets tough. They can make you laugh too.

PISCES *Sympathy, support, love.* These romantic lovers never let you down. They can take you with them into their personal fantasy world and they are always ready for a laugh.

WHICH SIGN ARE YOU COMPATIBLE WITH?

AQUARIUS/ARIES
A good combination as they have complementary characteristics.

AQUARIUS/TAURUS
Both stubborn and Taurus too slow for Aquarius.

AQUARIUS/GEMINI
Can work well, although Gemini may resent Aquarius sarcasm.

AQUARIUS/CANCER
Little in common and quite different in nature, not a good match.

AQUARIUS/LEO
Aquarius enjoys Leo's creativity, Leo enjoys Aquarius's wit.

AQUARIUS/VIRGO
Can work if the Virgoan doesn't need too much reassurance.

AQUARIUS/LIBRA
A good combination as long as the Aquarian enjoys sex.

AQUARIUS/SCORPIO
Both think they are right all the time, so not a good match.

AQUARIUS/SAGITTARIUS
Can be a good combination, especially when interests are shared.

AQUARIUS/CAPRICORN
Much in common so often a good match.

AQUARIUS/AQUARIUS
Anything can happen in this weird and wonderful match.

AQUARIUS/PISCES
Can work very well, as long as the Aquarian is caring enough.

Your Prospects for 1999

LOVE

Short-lived love affairs are unlikely this year but if you do find yourself attracted to someone new it is likely to be during April and May when Venus activated the fun and pleasure area of your horoscope. However, supposedly settled relationships, like just about everything else in your life this year, will be extremely unsettled for much of the time. You may be in the throes of moving from one relationship to another with all the attendant aggravation that that brings. You may think you have found just the right person to spend your life with, only to find that circumstances make this difficult. Love may come and go through your life like an express train this year. You may indeed be happily settled in a nice comfortable marriage, only to find that it is no longer as comfortable as you thought. There may even be absolutely no emotional difficulties between you and your lover but your circumstances of life may be in such an upheaval that your lives are disrupted. You and your lover may be intensely happy together but you could have still a lot to contend with but if you pull together and work to make each other happy, your love will stand the tests of this strange and difficult year. You and your partner will need a sense of humour this year, that's for sure. There are many planetary reasons for the dislocation of your lives but the eclipses of the 31st of January, the 16th of February, the 28th of July and the 11th of August will bring many problems to a head for both of you. If you happen to be living with a Leo partner, the problems will be even more amazing. Sasha and her husband are Leo and Aquarius, so good luck to us this year as well as to you!

MONEY AND WORK

Every part of your life will be unsettled this year and changes of job or major changes in your financial position are more than likely. If you have an ordinary job working for an ordinary organization, the chances are that changes in the way this is run will affect you from time to time. However, if you are in a working partnership or if you are self-employed, you can expect more than the usual number of problems and also of successes now. At least it won't be boring. However, this area of your life shows more steady growth and less chaos than the personal and domestic side of your life. Indeed, you can make progress at work throughout May, June, July and the middle of August than is usual. Financially, you have some excellent opportunities for windfalls or for gambles paying off from January to mid-February but after that things should be pretty much on an even keel with the exception of March and April which may be a rather expensive times for you. To be honest, you could do very well this year, especially if you follow hunches and take advantage of some of the strange and unusual opportunities that will arise for you this year.

HEALTH

Fortunately for you, with all the other difficulties you may face this year, you should be pretty fit most of the time. The only really awkward time will be early in August when an accident to your arms, hands or wrists may occur. Your own level of strength and energy will be pretty good for most of this year while the last few weeks of the year will find you at the peak of your strength and energy. You may be restless at times and you could find it hard to sleep from time to time, especially around the time of those eclipses. Older family members may become ill during March and April and again towards the end of the year but there seems to be plenty of help on hand for them if they find that they need it.

FAMILY AND HOME

Your domestic circumstances have been unsettled for some years past and the chances are that you have already moved house fairly recently but you may decide to make another move this year. Alternatively, you could acquire a second property or you could do some extensive work on the one you are living in now. Older family members will need some of your time and attention and father figures in particular may have bouts of illness or other problems that you have to attend to. Older females may need help during the last weeks of the year but up to then they seem to manage quite well. Children and youngsters pose no real problems this year.

LUCK

Your luck will be very up and down this year and there are likely to be so many unexpected events that it is terribly hard to tell just how things will go. However, there is an indication that events around your neighbourhood will work in your favour and it might be through local connections that you can make some very welcome extra cash. Brothers, sisters and other relatives of your own generation will prove to be very helpful to you. If you need a new vehicle this year, just the right thing could fall into your lap at just the right moment.

The Aspects and their Astrological Meanings

CONJUNCT	This shows important events which are usually, but not always, good.
SEXTILE	Good, particularly for work and mental activity.
SQUARE	Difficult, challenging.
TRINE	Great for romance, family life and creativity.
OPPOSITE	Awkward, depressing, challenging.
INTO	This shows when a particular planet enters a new sign of the zodiac, thus setting off a new phase or a new set of circumstances.
DIRECT	When a planet resumes normal direct motion.
RETROGRADE	When a planet apparently begins to go backwards.
VOID	When the Moon makes no aspect to any planet.

September at a Glance

LOVE	❤	❤	❤	❤	❤
WORK	★	★			
MONEY	£	£	£		
HEALTH	✪				
LUCK	♲	♲	♲		

TUESDAY, 1ST SEPTEMBER
Moon trine Saturn

The company of an elderly relative or friend will be pleasurable today. You will possibly discover something fascinating from your own or your family's past. The wealth of anecdotes that come your way will be simply amazing. Make sure you are suitably grateful.

WEDNESDAY, 2ND SEPTEMBER
Void Moon

The term 'void' of course means that neither the Moon nor any of the other planets is making any important aspects during the course of their travels. When this kind of day occurs, the worst thing you can do is to try to start something new or get anything important off the ground. Do nothing special today except for routine tasks.

THURSDAY, 3RD SEPTEMBER
Moon conjunct Neptune

A day of peace and quiet would do you no harm at all, which is a good thing since you'll be in the mood for contemplation. Gentle music and some solitude will suit you down to the ground. If you are artistically inclined, this is a good time to plan a new creative project.

FRIDAY, 4TH SEPTEMBER
Mars opposite Uranus

Although the actions of a partner or close friend annoy you today, it's not wise to give vent to an outburst of temper. That won't solve anything, and it could make things worse in the long run. We know that it's hard to be reasonable all the time, so perhaps the best solution is to avoid each other until you've got over your temper and cooled down.

SATURDAY, 5TH SEPTEMBER
Moon opposite Venus

Your own interests must take a back seat today, because your other half is in dire need of some tender loving care and attention. Get your priorities right and all will be well – there's nothing so vital that can't be put off for another day. Devote some time to the one who means the most to you. Even if you're single, there's a friend in need close at hand.

SUNDAY, 6TH SEPTEMBER
Full Moon eclipse

Today's eclipse of the Moon brings something to a head in connection with partnerships and relationships. Eclipses have had an unfortunate reputation ever since astrology began, and this probably goes back to a time long before man learned to record anything in writing. However, there are approximately two solar and two lunar eclipses each year, so remember that they are not so special, or so terrible.

MONDAY, 7TH SEPTEMBER
Moon sextile Neptune

Follow your nose to a bargain today. If you are determined to go on a shopping trip, you'll find that you can sniff out the cheapest and best like a bloodhound. Don't worry too much about the expense, because anything you purchase will be well worth the cost.

TUESDAY, 8TH SEPTEMBER
Mercury into Virgo

Secrets must be kept, that's the astral message when Mercury enters your solar house of intimate affairs from today. Those of you who are involved in clandestine relationships had better make sure that your personal security codes aren't breached. Confidences of all sorts, whether of a sexual or financial nature, must be guarded now. Let discretion be your watchword.

WEDNESDAY, 9TH SEPTEMBER
Mercury trine Saturn

This is an excellent time to seek advice on such things as mortgages, taxation, corporate matters and legacies, particularly if property is involved. A relative may wish to discuss a will or insurance agreement.

AQUARIUS

THURSDAY, 10TH SEPTEMBER
Venus trine Saturn

Thrift and economy are the buzzwords today, even though your financial fortunes are looking reasonably good at the moment. Just because some extra cash is likely to come in doesn't mean that you should immediately splash out! Be sensible and budget carefully.

FRIDAY, 11TH SEPTEMBER
Mercury conjunct Venus

You have the ability to charm the birds from the trees and, better still, to charm your lover into doing almost anything that you want. Take some time off to talk, make love or simply enjoy being together.

SATURDAY, 12TH SEPTEMBER
Moon sextile Mars

Stave off the dreaded encroachment of boredom and whisk your lover off to paint the town red. Your lover will find it hard to keep up with you today, but at least they won't find you dull! Singles will find going out and about even more productive, because today is the day when you may discover the love of your life.

SUNDAY, 13TH SEPTEMBER
Moon square Jupiter

Children could cause you extra expense at the moment, and you may need to spend the cash you had put by for small luxuries on youngsters. Alternatively, a creative venture or sporting hobby could cost more than you had bargained for.

MONDAY, 14TH SEPTEMBER
Moon sextile Venus

Your partner may surprise you by giving you a really great welcome home. He or she may have the washing done, the dinner in the oven, a bottle of wine cooling in the fridge and a lovely smile to greet you. There may be good news for either or both of you which brings you closer to achieving a shared goal. A woman could be helpful and even inspirational in connection with work.

TUESDAY, 15TH SEPTEMBER
Moon sextile Sun

The more normal and undemanding the day the better, as far as you're concerned. You won't want to stray too far from the straight and narrow, and you certainly won't want to immerse yourself in the madding (and maddening) throng!

AQUARIUS

WEDNESDAY, 16TH SEPTEMBER
Sun opposite Jupiter

Your expectations are high today, but the true picture is unpromising. You may think that you've got plenty of cash to play with, but regret it when the credit card bill comes in. We know you enjoy the finer things in life, but don't knock your budget out for a month by being such a spendthrift. It's said that the best things in life are free, so you don't really have to go overboard to enjoy yourself.

THURSDAY, 17TH SEPTEMBER
Moon conjunct Mars

This is a great day for lovers! Whether your relationship is new or if you have been with your partner for years, there will be more than a touch of romance in the air. You seem to be full of exciting plans for the future, and you could both be excited about an event that affects you as a couple.

FRIDAY, 18TH SEPTEMBER
Moon trine Saturn

Your parents could help you out in a big way today. They may be happy to lend you something that you need, or to come and help out with a household problem. People in positions of responsibility will be quite impressed by your intelligence and ability.

SATURDAY, 19TH SEPTEMBER
Mercury opposite Jupiter

There could be disturbing news about a business or money matter today. Travel plans may have to be delayed, possibly due to lack of funds. You should take extra care while driving now. In short, keep your mind on what you are doing, because you may be easily distracted.

SUNDAY, 20TH SEPTEMBER
New Moon

Today's New Moon forecasts a new start in one of the most intimate areas of your horoscope. It's your chance to review your personal life and expectations. Past emotional hurts can now be put behind you, giving you room to look to the future with more confidence. Financial affairs, too, come under scrutiny, because you're in the right frame of mind to sort out any muddle, whether monetary or romantic.

MONDAY, 21ST SEPTEMBER
Moon sextile Pluto

You may be able to persuade others to do what you want today, but you could have to pay them back by doing what they want on another occasion. An inheritance could also be on the cards now, in the form of a legacy or a small windfall of another kind.

TUESDAY, 22ND SEPTEMBER
Sun trine Neptune

A solar aspect to Neptune isn't usually good news for your cash, but today is the exception. Take note of your hunches and intuition – you're bound to be right, and they'll lead you to profit. In more personal matters, your sensitivity will win the trust of someone very special.

WEDNESDAY, 23RD SEPTEMBER
Sun into Libra

Today the Sun moves into your house of philosophy, beliefs and travel, broadening your mental and physical horizons over the next month. This area of your horoscope is associated with adventure, and may actually deal with journeys to distant and exotic parts of the world. Tempting as that idea may seem, the truth is likely to be closer to home. It's a time to indulge your curiosity, and you'll embark upon a journey within your own mind to explore religious or spiritual issues. Many of you will wish to enter a more academic field, so examine the possibility of college courses and other forms of adult education.

THURSDAY, 24TH SEPTEMBER
Mercury into Libra

Mercury enters the most philosophical area of your chart today, and this is an opportunity for intellectual growth. Many of your past beliefs will fall by the wayside as you find other concepts that fit more logically into your life. Positive thinking is important, as you'll realize it's only negativity that has held you back. The academically inclined should do well under this influence. The tiny planet also gives a boost to your travel prospects.

FRIDAY, 25TH SEPTEMBER
Sun conjunct Mercury

This is a day when your strong feelings about religion or politics will be expressed forcefully but persuasively. There's nothing you like better than reasoned argument. And by that, we mean an argument you can win! Of course, not everyone will fall in line with your thinking immediately, but you're on your way to gaining a few converts. This is also an excellent day for embarking on a voyage of discovery – both physical and mental.

SATURDAY, 26TH SEPTEMBER
Moon conjunct Pluto

Beware of a nag who won't give you any peace. It's the fault of the Moon and Pluto, putting insistent thoughts in the mind of a friend. Okay, so your companion only wants the best for you, but you could do without the intensity and browbeating. Of course there may be something in this for him or her too, but at least your pal does have your best interests at heart.

SUNDAY, 27TH SEPTEMBER
Mercury sextile Pluto

You're in quite a philosophical mood today, ready and able to discuss the most profound concepts in depth. A like-minded person will be a pleasure to talk to, and you'll find that their opinions will give you food for thought.

MONDAY, 28TH SEPTEMBER
Moon trine Saturn

You may be dreaming about the kind of home you would like to live in. While it may not be possible to have what you want now, there does seem to be a chance that you will get it in the long run. Turn your thoughts to practical schemes to make this possible.

TUESDAY, 29TH SEPTEMBER
Sun sextile Pluto

A hope that you've had for some time will come a step nearer to fulfilment today. You may have had to keep this quiet for a while, but eventually all will be revealed and then you'll have a cause to celebrate.

WEDNESDAY, 30TH SEPTEMBER
Venus into Libra

Everything seems a bit dull and mundane to you to today, and your rather restless mood will make you yearn to visit far-flung places. If your lover suggests that you start planning a trip, you'll jump at the idea. Practical matters, such as whether you can afford it or if you can actually manage to get away when you want to, will be beside the point.

October at a Glance

LOVE	❤	❤	❤	❤	
WORK	★	★	★	★	
MONEY	£	£	£	£	
HEALTH	✚	✚	✚		
LUCK	♘	♘	♘	♘	♘

THURSDAY, 1ST OCTOBER
Sun trine Uranus

The Sun unites with your ruling planet, Uranus, to open your eyes and mind to the numerous possibilities surrounding you. Your thoughts will tend to the more unconventional and original. If you're artistically inclined, then there's an air of genius about you now. You may come across someone whose views you don't share, but with whom you achieve a remarkable understanding.

FRIDAY, 2ND OCTOBER
Moon opposite Mars

There is a great deal of activity going on throughout this month in the relationship area of your chart, and fortunately most of it will be favourable. However, there are bound to be a few hiccups and teething troubles, and today will be one of those days. You may not be able to say the right thing to others or someone else may get on your nerves. The chances are that the person who upsets you is a man.

SATURDAY, 3RD OCTOBER
Moon square Pluto

Although a friend may come to you with a financial proposal that puts you into the high-income bracket on sight, don't be too ready to fall in with a scheme that may be nothing more than pie-in-the-sky. We know you won't want to pour cold water on any aspirations, but we doubt that the sums will actually add up. Err on the side of caution in all monetary matters today.

SUNDAY, 4TH OCTOBER
Moon conjunct Jupiter

The Moon links up with lucky Jupiter today in your solar house of cash! That's got to mean good fortune when it comes to material concerns. Money-making opportunities are all around, and if you decide to spend cash rather than make it you'll find plenty of bargains.

MONDAY, 5TH OCTOBER
Venus sextile Pluto

A close friend may wish to get even closer under the intense influence of Pluto and the romantic vibes of Venus. This is fine if you're single and agreeable, but if there are relationship complications on either side then you'd be wise to think again before you get in too deep. You'll have to be firm yet tactful to extricate yourself without bruising tender feelings.

TUESDAY, 6TH OCTOBER
Full Moon

The Full Moon puts the spotlight on your intellectual abilities. You may feel that you want to improve your qualifications, and if so then this is the perfect time to find out more about courses in your area. On the other hand, the whole issue of past assumptions and convictions could be called into question. Mentally this is a challenging time, but it just goes to show that you're never too old to learn something new.

WEDNESDAY, 7TH OCTOBER
Mars into Virgo

Your financial position is set to improve now. You will soon be able to recoup previous losses and put yourself back in the black. You may be in the early stages of a new relationship or partnership, and settling down will probably take more adjustment than you had bargained for.

THURSDAY, 8TH OCTOBER
Moon sextile Jupiter

Financially this should be a good day. We're not promising a windfall, but if you've got any big plans for your home, such as redecoration, new furnishings, an extension or even changing your abode totally, you'll find that the cash is there if you use your head. You're certainly shrewd enough to work out a suitable strategy, and luck is with you.

FRIDAY, 9TH OCTOBER
Moon trine Uranus

If you're a person who has always been sure about rights and wrongs, taste and decorum, you could be in for something of a shock today. Your eyes will be open to other possibilities, so some of your well-established views will undergo a swift review. Don't cling to convention, because this enlightenment is a sign of your personal development.

SATURDAY, 10TH OCTOBER
Mars trine Saturn

Financial matters are highlighted again this week. Today you may need to take some kind of professional or specialist advice, especially in connection with mortgages, property matters, legacies, wills, taxation, corporate or family issues that pertain to money.

SUNDAY, 11TH OCTOBER
Neptune direct

Neptune returns to a more direct course from today, bringing an almost psychic awareness into your life. From now on, spare some time to listen to the inner voice of intuition. It won't let you down, even if it does conflict with sober logic from time to time.

MONDAY, 12TH OCTOBER
Mercury into Scorpio

Today, Mercury enters your solar tenth house of aims and ambitions. You can now keep your eye firmly fixed on your goals and know you have a fair chance of achieving them. This is a time to speak up and make your views known to those who matter. People in authority will be impressed by your candour.

TUESDAY, 13TH OCTOBER
Moon square Mercury

It's a pity that when the Moon makes a bad aspect to Mercury you can't seem to say the right thing. No matter what the topic, those around you seem determined to misunderstand your point of view. If you want any peace now, keep your lips sealed because you'll get very little sympathy or understanding. The trouble is that you are pretty logical while those around you are too emotional to see anything clearly.

WEDNESDAY, 14TH OCTOBER
Mercury sextile Mars

You'll find yourself in a very decisive frame of mind today. You'll be capable of anything and feel secure, no matter what the world throws at you. There may be some who criticize, but you won't feel a thing.

A Q U A R I U S

THURSDAY, 15TH OCTOBER
Moon trine Saturn

It's a difficult day, but one that has to be faced if you're to put old irritations behind you once and for all. Some duties have to be dealt with, and you can't put them off any longer. The best advice is to get your head down and race through it as quickly as possible. This way, the painful experience will be over as soon as possible. Difficult forms and documents will play a major part in all this, so pay attention to the small print.

FRIDAY, 16TH OCTOBER
Moon square Pluto

Suspicions are aroused by the strange actions of a friend. Before you jump to conclusions, it would be wise to try to find out more about the supposed motives and consequences of your friend's activities. This could be disquieting, especially if money has a part to play, but keep your patience. All will be revealed in time.

SATURDAY, 17TH OCTOBER
Mercury square Uranus

Disturbing news today could put you in a whirl, but the situation probably isn't as dire as you imagine! Don't over-react now – just wait, and all will become clear when someone cracks under the strain of keeping a secret!

SUNDAY, 18TH OCTOBER
Uranus direct

As a restatement of your newly found confidence Uranus, ruler of your sign, resumes a direct course, banishing indecision and insecurity. It may be the latter part of the year, yet there's a need for a spring clean. You'll now be prepared to ditch a lot of the past and abandon those rigid concepts that have held you back. You might even develop an interest in high fashion.

MONDAY, 19TH OCTOBER
Mars square Pluto

Past sins, or those things considered to be sins, are set to catch up with you today. The influence of Mars and Pluto tends to encourage envy, so watch your back! If there was a day to have a bad turn done to you, unfortunately this is it. Of course, if you face up to these problems you could defuse a potentially explosive situation. Take heart, for all is not lost.

AQUARIUS

TUESDAY, 20TH OCTOBER
New Moon

Today's New Moon certainly indicates a new start for you. You're filled to the brim with good ideas and your mind is working overtime. If there's been a subject that has interested you for some time, this could be your chance to learn more, and possibly gain a qualification. Educational matters are favoured now, as indeed is anything that increases your knowledge and experience. A stimulating conversation will point the way forward.

WEDNESDAY, 21ST OCTOBER
Moon square Uranus

Would you like a day off? No such luck, we're afraid, for the tense aspect between the Moon and Uranus may disrupt your peace of mind. It could be that you are carrying far too many work worries home, or the burden of an elderly relative is proving too pressing. Fretting doesn't work, so try to approach problems in a calmer frame of mind.

THURSDAY, 22ND OCTOBER
Sun square Neptune

The stars are not doing much of anything today, so if you can make it a day of rest, you'll be doing yourself a favour. You could spend a bit of time looking at travel brochures and picking out somewhere nice to go later in the year, or you could benefit by reading or studying.

FRIDAY, 23RD OCTOBER
Sun into Scorpio

Career affairs are in the spotlight now, so concentrate on where you are going and make an effort to impress the right people over the next few weeks. Forget about romance for a while – keep your eye on the business and financial goals instead.

SATURDAY, 24TH OCTOBER
Venus into Scorpio

A woman could be instrumental in helping you to achieve one of your most deeply held ambitions today and, what is more, this help could come completely out of the blue. This friend or colleague will put herself out for no reason other than that of fostering your talent or helping you on your way. A sudden and unexpected social invitation could come through work, and this is so favourable that you really must accept.

AQUARIUS

SUNDAY, 25TH OCTOBER
Saturn into Aries retrograde

Saturn's return to an intellectual area of your chart may indicate a need to improve some of your qualifications or prompt the undertaking of a course of study. Don't be nervous about this, because your mental powers will certainly meet the challenge.

MONDAY, 26TH OCTOBER
Sun conjunct Venus

You're in a far more influential position than you realize! The conjunction of the Sun and Venus ensures that you present the most pleasing side of your personality. Charm oozes from every pore and your smile is to die for. If you've got any professional or personal favours to ask, this is the day to do it! Your charisma makes refusal impossible.

TUESDAY, 27TH OCTOBER
Moon sextile Mercury

Troubles at work seem to be getting themselves sorted out, and it may be that a female colleague or boss is helping you to do this. Your health is improving, and you should feel less tired and washed-out. You should hear some interesting and amusing news or gossip from a strange or unusual source today.

WEDNESDAY, 28TH OCTOBER
Moon square Sun

A world-weary mood takes a hold under a harsh lunar aspect to the Sun today. You've put up with a lot of pressures recently, and even though the more general outlook is good you are showing the strain. People's expectations could be a major part of the problem. You've done a lot for others recently, but you could honestly do with a day off.

THURSDAY, 29TH OCTOBER
Saturn square Neptune

The vague feeling that 'there's got to be something more to life than this' is the feature of the day. The combined influences of Saturn and Neptune tend to promote unease, and this will affect your thinking profoundly. Don't allow this disquiet to descend into despondency. Think positive!

FRIDAY, 30TH OCTOBER
Moon sextile Saturn

You're in a very serious frame of mind today. The Moon aspects Saturn, and this inclines your thoughts to serious topics and away from light-hearted people. Unfortunately, your sense of humour is a casualty of this sobering influence, so try to ease up just a little. We know that at times the world may hold little to laugh at, but at least try to smile… it makes everything so much more bearable.

SATURDAY, 31ST OCTOBER
Moon conjunct Jupiter

Money-wise this is an extremely fortunate day, for the giant planet, Jupiter, is activated and will shower good fortune on anything to do with your finances. An act of kindness will go a long way, for what you give you'll receive a hundredfold in return. You'll express Jupiter's generosity now.

November at a Glance

LOVE	❤			
WORK	★	★	★	★
MONEY	£	£	£	
HEALTH	✪	✪		
LUCK	ʊ	ʊ	ʊ	

SUNDAY, 1ST NOVEMBER
Mercury into Sagittarius

The charitable impulses that make you such an endearing soul could become a liability just now. Mercury moves into your eleventh solar house, making you the target for every plausible rogue with a story of woe. You are more than prepared to help, but make sure that any cause you support is genuine. At least you're assured of a convivial atmosphere with friends over the next few weeks.

MONDAY, 2ND NOVEMBER
Void Moon

There are no important planetary aspects today and even the Moon is unaspected. This kind of a day is called a 'void of course Moon' day. The best way to approach such a day is to do what is normal and natural for you without starting anything new or important.

AQUARIUS

TUESDAY, 3RD NOVEMBER
Moon square Neptune

You won't be at your most organized today. A day trip may have to be postponed or even cancelled. However, you won't much care since almost any activity will be too much trouble at the moment. Take to your bed if you feel like it – you may as well laze the time away, since you won't be able to get anything going anyway!

WEDNESDAY, 4TH NOVEMBER
Full Moon

Today's Full Moon puts the spotlight on your career. There have been a lot of changes both around you and within yourself. Now you have to decide exactly what you want, and in which direction to proceed. Before you can act, you need a carefully thought-out plan, so take time to ensure that strategies for progress are workable. Authority figures will be impressed by your determination.

THURSDAY, 5TH NOVEMBER
Moon trine Neptune

A misty look is apparent in your eye as a dreamy frame of mind overtakes the more common-sense aspects of your personality. You'll feel extremely nostalgic, and content to dwell on your rose-tinted, happy memories.

FRIDAY, 6TH NOVEMBER
Mercury conjunct Pluto

Your views and personality will have a profound effect on someone today – whether you know it or not. In fact, you'll be amazed to discover just how influential your opinions are.

SATURDAY, 7TH NOVEMBER
Mars opposite Jupiter

A man seems to be making a point of behaving in an awkward and obstructive manner towards you today. You and a partner or close associate may disagree over the way you spend your money.

SUNDAY, 8TH NOVEMBER
Venus trine Jupiter

Any aspect between Venus and Jupiter tends to enhance your popularity, and give a helping hand to your love life, too. Today though, the outlook also promotes more practical concerns. In money matters and career, the two fortunate planets show that with a little charm you can get your own way. If you're asking for loans, a favour or even a promotion, it would be hard to refuse you.

AQUARIUS

MONDAY, 9TH NOVEMBER
Venus sextile Mars

Your initiative, charm and undoubted sex appeal combine to ease your path through all sorts of business and financial complications today. You can solve a lot of problems with a smile backed up by considerable determination. A newcomer to the workplace could awaken a romantic interest.

TUESDAY, 10TH NOVEMBER
Sun trine Jupiter

There are a number of opportunities around you at the moment, and you should take full advantage of this favourable trend. You may have to make some kind of adjustment to your aims and ambitions soon.

WEDNESDAY, 11TH NOVEMBER
Moon square Venus

There are so many planetary influences today that you won't know which way to turn! You may know that your thinking is right, but it could be impossible to influence others or to convince them that you know what you're doing. You may come up against officious types who make it their business to give you a hard time, or even experience unkindness or sarcasm from another quarter.

THURSDAY, 12TH NOVEMBER
Moon square Pluto

A friend may do or say something that is out of character today, which will make you wonder if you're being deceived. You may conclude that there's far more going on behind the scenes than you had suspected. If you sense this, it's best to steer clear of the situation.

FRIDAY, 13TH NOVEMBER
Jupiter direct

Jupiter returns to a more direct motion today, bringing luck to bear on your material concerns from now on. Any delays in connection with payments owed or any other kind of money matter will soon be resolved to your advantage

SATURDAY, 14TH NOVEMBER
Sun sextile Mars

If you set a steady course now towards achieving your aims and ambitions, you should be able to reach your destination quite easily. Maybe you have an exam looming, or perhaps you are trying to finish some kind of outdoor chore while the weather is good enough? Whatever it is, you will achieve your goal in the end.

AQUARIUS

SUNDAY, 15TH NOVEMBER
Moon sextile Mercury

You're terribly restless today and can't wait to get away from the jaded and familiar. Although your basic inclinations may be to travel as far away as you can, you'd be the first to admit that it's not always possible. If you are chained to the domestic or work scene, then you need something to take your mind off the usual affairs of your life. A good conversation, a fascinating book or absorbing television show should improve your mood.

MONDAY, 16TH NOVEMBER
Moon opposite Saturn

If you're off on your travels today then be prepared to put up with some delays and detours along the way. Nothing really can go exactly to schedule at the moment, since the stressful influence of Saturn is out to disrupt your well-ordered plans. Difficulties must be borne with patience.

TUESDAY, 17TH NOVEMBER
Venus into Sagittarius

Venus, planet of harmony, enters your solar area of friendships from today, starting a period of social activities, fun and new encounters. Romance and social life mingle now, so at the very least this will be a month of flirtation. An old friend may also be seen in a new and more intimate light. If you have any artistic aspirations, you should follow your instincts because the influence of Venus is excellent for anything to do with flair and originality.

WEDNESDAY, 18TH NOVEMBER
Moon trine Jupiter

This should be a very optimistic and outgoing day. The lunar aspect to Jupiter gives you an abundance of good luck, especially concerning money and business dealings. Be prepared for opportunity to knock and react immediately, because you can't really go wrong when the heavens smile on all your endeavours.

THURSDAY, 19TH NOVEMBER
New Moon

Your career gets a kick start from the New Moon today. For many this heralds the start of a new job, for others a chance to branch out on your own. Good luck! Not that you'll really need it, of course, because you'll be go-getting, enterprising and shrewd. Show the world that you're a real whizz-kid!

AQUARIUS

FRIDAY, 20TH NOVEMBER
Mercury square Jupiter

Sometimes when among friends you can get carried away by your eloquence…
and some of the statements you're making today are exaggerated, to say the least!
The trouble is that you're being egged on. Try to moderate your patter, otherwise
you'll look something of a fool when the time comes to prove your claims. Don't
talk yourself into a financial commitment that you won't be able to back out of.

SATURDAY, 21ST NOVEMBER
Mercury retrograde

Mercury has turned to retrograde motion for the time being, and this always
brings muddles and misunderstandings. Mercury is concerned with
communication in all forms, so when it is retrograde important pieces of paper
go missing, cheques get lost and phone calls and messages don't reach their
destination. Travel can also be awkward at such times.

SUNDAY, 22ND NOVEMBER
Sun into Sagittarius

The Sun's progress into your solar area of hopes, wishes and ideals shows that
the ball's in your court now. You have all the facts and figures at your disposal,
you've thought your prospects through and now it's up to you to start to make
your dreams come true. There are risks, we admit, but if you really want
something then make some positive moves towards attaining it. Good friends will
be of enormous help at this time. Be independent and self-motivated, you'll
receive all the backing you need; just have the courage of your convictions. Venus,
too, lends a helping hand, ensuring that luck is on your side.

MONDAY, 23RD NOVEMBER
Venus conjunct Pluto

You exert a powerful spell today. The conjunction of Venus and Pluto accents
your sexuality, and the effect that you have on those around you will be
devastating! You may think that this is an overstatement, but it's not so. Someone
close will happily sweep you off your feet, given half a chance.

TUESDAY, 24TH NOVEMBER
Moon sextile Sun

This is a fortunate day on which the rays of the moon and sun mingle to bring
you happy times in the company of friends. It could be that someone around you
has had a stroke of luck and wishes to share this with you.

AQUARIUS

WEDNESDAY, 25TH NOVEMBER
Venus sextile Uranus

Social gatherings of any sort become the arena for you to display your charm and powers of attraction. You could be surprised by the obvious response you get to your flirtatious games. You might not even mean to attract such attention, but attract it you will!

THURSDAY, 26TH NOVEMBER
Moon sextile Saturn

You do have sound common sense, but it's not always a quality that's understood by those who are more flighty. You're determined to make the best of new opportunities, but those around you may not fully understand the scope of your plans. You are well aware that sacrifices will have to be made to make your dreams come true, so if you explain the reasons behind your sober attitudes you'll win more appreciation for your efforts.

FRIDAY, 27TH NOVEMBER
Neptune into Aquarius

Neptune, watery planet of inspiration, moves into your sign today. Although you may find yourself prone to confusion for a while, this planet's lessons show that you should use your intuition more and not rely on logic alone to chart your course through life.

SATURDAY, 28TH NOVEMBER
Mars trine Neptune

If you go out of your way to help someone who is down on their luck today, you will feel good about yourself. You may visit a sick friend or give a helping hand to someone who needs it in a practical way, but you could also give some counselling and advice to someone who needs a friend to talk things over with. Your partner will be full of energy, and he or she will be able to give you a hand if you are overloaded with chores.

SUNDAY, 29TH NOVEMBER
Sun conjunct Pluto

The intense conjunction between the Sun and Pluto could bring things to a head where friendships are concerned. They'll continue on a new footing, or you'll feel that you have to abandon them for something better. Either way, the choice is yours.

MONDAY, 30TH NOVEMBER
Moon conjunct Saturn

The Moon teams up with Saturn today, endowing you with considerable self discipline and a capacity for hard work. You have the ability to sit down and concentrate deeply now, and no problem is beyond you. In social interactions, a more serious side to your character will emerge.

December at a Glance

LOVE	❤	❤	❤	❤	
WORK	★	★			
MONEY	£	£	£		
HEALTH	✛	✛	✛	✛	✛
LUCK	♘	♘	♘		

TUESDAY, 1ST DECEMBER
Mercury sextile Uranus

You seem to be surrounded by eccentric people at the moment, and you're enjoying every minute of it! You're in a very open-minded mood now, so any suggestions or ideas your friends make will get a fair hearing and a new concept could make you think deeply about your beliefs. Spontaneous fun is on offer, as well as food for thought.

WEDNESDAY, 2ND DECEMBER
Sun sextile Uranus

This should be an exciting day when new things and people are going to enter your life and change it for the better. The Sun positively aspects Uranus now, urging you to seek out new friends. This is no time to be a wallflower. Go out and enjoy yourself! You'll find dazzling company and a lot of laughs.

THURSDAY, 3RD DECEMBER
Full Moon

An emotional problem seems to be coming to a head now and it will need a practical solution. You may find that one of your children behaves in a way that is out of character, or he or she suddenly becomes unmanageable for a while. You will need to do some investigation into this before working out the best way of tackling the problem. A lover could suddenly spring a totally unexpected tantrum on you, too.

FRIDAY, 4TH DECEMBER
Moon opposite Venus

There's an action-packed sky today with the main accent on your ambitions. You may be dissatisfied with your present career, or feel that you aren't getting sufficient financial rewards for your efforts. A friend could suggest a course of action that boosts your self-esteem. Consider all advice, because many opportunities lay ahead.

SATURDAY, 5TH DECEMBER
Mercury sextile Mars

A friend's suggestion for a holiday or a short break away from routine should be seriously considered today. You know that the change would do you good, so what's holding you back? If you think that money constraints could halt the idea, think again – after all, where there's a will, there's a way!

SUNDAY, 6TH DECEMBER
Moon trine Jupiter

You may be asked to travel in connection with your work today and the outcome of all this could be quite exciting. It seems that there are some really good money-making opportunities on the way to you now, too. Contact with new people and innovative working methods will be important at this time.

MONDAY, 7TH DECEMBER
Moon sextile Mars

A man whom you live or work with will come up with some really useful ideas today, and these may provide the answer to a number of tricky problems that have troubled you lately. There could be some great news about money, and this will set you and your lover thinking about the best way to use it. Help and co-operation from other people will be just the thing to put you back on the right track.

TUESDAY, 8TH DECEMBER
Moon trine Sun

Today the Moon is in splendid aspect to the Sun, making this a day of good fortune and exuberance. Harmony in close relationships is forecast, as well as a happy social event. Friends are extra supportive and helpful, and generally fun to be around.

WEDNESDAY, 9TH DECEMBER
Venus trine Saturn

When Venus and Saturn gang up, remember that flippant attitudes and remarks can be banished if you respond carefully. A serious emotional commitment may also be necessary now. Think deeply about your feelings and about the way you want a romance to go, because a lot will rest on today's decision.

THURSDAY, 10TH DECEMBER
Moon square Sun

You can be quite secretive at times, so don't be too surprised if friends get suspicious about your motives. Whatever they are, you'll feel that it's your business, not theirs! The more inquisitive people around you become, the more defensive you'll be. Remember that you too can be prone to the odd unfounded suspicion.

FRIDAY, 11TH DECEMBER
Venus into Capricorn

Venus moves into your solar twelfth house today, bringing a period of reflection and retreat. You may not want to do much socializing over the next month and you may not feel up to doing anything energetic. You seem to want your own company or, perhaps, the company of one trusted friend. Oddly enough, romantic matters and even out-and-out love affairs will prosper now, as long as you keep them quiet for the time being.

SATURDAY, 12TH DECEMBER
Mars sextile Pluto

Be ready for action today! A friend may come up with a novel suggestion that you'd be advised to agree to immediately. If this involves going somewhere different, it will prove to be a very enjoyable time. New people are out there waiting to meet you, so hit the social scene with a vengeance!

SUNDAY, 13TH DECEMBER
Moon sextile Sun

You'll feel the urge to forget tradition and strike out on a new and independent course today. Travel seems very appealing now, especially if you've been under pressure from your in-laws, so any time away should be welcome.

MONDAY, 14TH DECEMBER
Moon sextile Venus

The Moon's pleasing contact with Venus reminds you that you have so many friends that some of them get left behind or tend to fall by the wayside as you make your path through life. Perhaps it's time you made the effort to get in contact again? If this involves travel – even foreign travel – then you can be sure of an abundant welcome.

TUESDAY, 15TH DECEMBER
Mars trine Uranus

You're at your most original and inventive today under the light of Mars and Uranus. The novel and exciting has plenty of appeal, and you'll be keen to savour the new experiences that the day brings. The thought of a vacation in an unknown part of the world among people of different cultures is stimulating, so act on your impulses and make a break for an exotic location.

WEDNESDAY, 16TH DECEMBER
Moon sextile Neptune

After yesterday's impulsiveness, this is a day for laying plans and working out subtle strategies. Don't allow yourself to be pressured into making sudden moves in any area, especially in the workplace. Think carefully before you act.

THURSDAY, 17TH DECEMBER
Moon sextile Uranus

It's time to forget your work worries and be sociable for once! You may have been neglecting the lighter, more pleasurable side of life, so now's your chance to put that right. Your friends have been wondering what's happened to you, so pop around and satisfy their justifiable curiosity.

FRIDAY, 18TH DECEMBER
New Moon

It's time to show the world what you're made of! The New Moon gives you the chance to show that you've got all the initiative and guts that you need to push a project through to a successful conclusion. Anything that requires personal flair combined with the co-operation of colleagues will go well. Don't be afraid to make your mark; you can do anything you set your mind to, so believe in yourself.

SATURDAY, 19TH DECEMBER
Sun trine Saturn

A great weight will be lifted from your shoulders today, and many of the worries you've recently experienced will be proved false. Positive thinking now takes centre stage, and you'll certainly notice the difference!

AQUARIUS

SUNDAY, 20TH DECEMBER
Moon square Mars

Watch your health today and take care not to have silly accidents. You may just do something stupid through fatigue or lack of concentration now. You may also have to watch what you say, because you could reveal a secret. If you're in the mood to drift and dream, cold reality will make it almost impossible.

MONDAY, 21ST DECEMBER
Mercury conjunct Pluto

There's a subtle change in the way you're thinking. Things you once desired no longer hold the same appeal, and new dreams are forming. Give it some thought, because with effort you can achieve every one of them.

TUESDAY, 22ND DECEMBER
Sun into Capricorn

The movement of the Sun into your solar twelfth house suggests that the next month may be rather solitary. You may be quite busy on a day-to-day basis, but behind this lies a need to retreat into yourself and reflect upon your progress. This is a wonderful time to repay anything owed to others, in the form of money, goods or obligations.

WEDNESDAY, 23RD DECEMBER
Mercury sextile Uranus

The Christmas spirit will be all around you today as the merry planet Mercury gets an adenaline boost from Uranus. Literally anything could happen when it comes to your social life! Your bubbly mood will be infectious, and you'll enjoy making new friends and being the centre of attention.

THURSDAY, 24TH DECEMBER
Moon square Pluto

The lunar aspect to Pluto is a little alarming for your bank balance today. You'd be well advised to look over the facts and figures because there's been an error made somewhere, and you can't afford to ignore it even though it's Christmas Eve! At least you can get to the bottom of this little mystery, but until you do you won't get much peace. In dealings with friends, tact and subtlety are important if you don't want to hurt their feelings.

FRIDAY, 25TH DECEMBER
Moon conjunct Jupiter

You can't even take a day off for Christmas, it seems, because this could be a red-letter day as far as financial matters are concerned. You could also be gratified to learn that other people share your outlook and understand your objectives in life. You may want to form a partnership for some reason now, and this too is well starred.

SATURDAY, 26TH DECEMBER
Moon square Sun

Other people are amazingly keen to remind you of things that you haven't done or jobs you haven't finished, and their bossy and interfering attitude is likely to drive you to distraction today. Just get on with what you have to do and tell your nagging friend or relative to get lost!

SUNDAY, 27TH DECEMBER
Moon square Venus

People of your sign are noted for a vivid, and sometimes unruly, imagination. In fact, you are sometimes more comfortable in the inner world of dreams and fantasy than you are in the all-too-solid world of harsh reality. Today is a case in point; you'd far rather drift along in a cloud of illusion, but the world does have a tendency to intrude. If you really want some peace to dream, then you'll have to pretend to be out. It should be quite easy – after all, you're good at pretending.

MONDAY, 28TH DECEMBER
Mercury sextile Mars

A friend may pop up out of the blue with just the answers you need to the questions that are bothering you most. You may be keen to put your personal philosophy of life into action today, and the world seems keen to help you do this.

TUESDAY, 29TH DECEMBER
Saturn direct

Your mind should be much clearer as Saturn resumes direct motion today. Your determination to improve your knowledge or qualifications will be enhanced, and any matters pertaining to education or transport should now run more smoothly.

WEDNESDAY, 30TH DECEMBER
Moon trine Neptune

The events of the day will prove that a lot of those things that you've taken for granted, perhaps for years, are falling away from you now. The Moon's aspect to Neptune encourages you to trust to your instincts and follow a course that isn't totally reliant on observable facts. This is particularly true of all creative ventures and in the area of romance. An infatuation is on the cards for many.

THURSDAY, 31ST DECEMBER
Moon trine Mars

The last day of the year sees you in a party mood. You'd rather be happily engaged in stimulating conversation with your friends than getting on with your daily tasks. Unfortunately, some things cannot be put off, but we think we can guarantee an enjoyable evening!

1999

January at a Glance

LOVE	♥	♥	♥	♥	♥
WORK	★				
MONEY	£	£	£		
HEALTH	⊕	⊕			
LUCK	∪	∪	∪		

FRIDAY, 1ST JANUARY
Mercury square Jupiter

Sometimes you can get carried away by your own eloquence amongst your friends. Some of the claims you're making as the year begins are exaggerated to say the least. The trouble is that you're being egged on. Try to moderate your speech otherwise you'll look something of a fool when the time comes to back up your words. Don't talk yourself into a financial commitment that you won't be able to back out of.

SATURDAY, 2ND JANUARY
Full Moon

Something is coming to a head in relation to your job. This is not a major crisis and there is absolutely no need to flounce out of a perfectly good job, but there is a problem that should be solved before you can continue on in a happy and peaceful frame of mind. You may have to sort out what your role is and which part of the job other people should be doing, because it looks as if you are carrying too much of the load at the moment.

AQUARIUS

SUNDAY, 3RD JANUARY
Moon opposite Venus

If your approach to health care involves lots of tasty treats and a somnolent spell stretched out on the sofa, that's all very well, but you know your body needs a spot more physical exercise and discipline to keep it in tip-top shape. Dietary indulgence is your particular bugbear, and today you need to be more than usually vigilant or you'll find your hand in that biscuit tin before you realize it!

MONDAY, 4TH JANUARY
Venus into Aquarius

The luxury loving planet, Venus, is suggesting that this is a great time to spoil yourself and also to enjoy yourself. So treat yourself to something nice and new that is for you alone. A new outfit would be a good idea or a few nice-smelling toiletries. Throw a party for your favourite friends and don't look the other way if someone seems to be fancying you.

TUESDAY, 5TH JANUARY
Venus conjunct Neptune

You won't know what it is that you've done but whatever it is, you've certainly found favour in the eyes of your loved ones. In fact those closest to you won't be able to do enough to please you. Before this treatment goes to your head, are you sure that you aren't being buttered up to do a favour or to be kept in the dark about some embarrassing news? You've usually got a keen eye for this sort of thing, so be blunt and ask what exactly is going on!

WEDNESDAY, 6TH JANUARY
Moon square Pluto

Suspicions are aroused by the strange actions of a friend today. Before you jump to conclusions it would be wise to try to find out more about the supposed motives and consequences of your friend's activities. This could be a disquieting time especially if money is involved in this web somewhere, but keep your patience. All will be revealed in time.

THURSDAY, 7TH JANUARY
Mercury into Capricorn

You'll find yourself in a more introspective mood for a few weeks because Mercury, planet of the mind enters the most secret and inward-looking portion of your horoscope from today. This is the start of a period when you'll want to understand the inner being, your own desires and motivations. Too much hectic life will prove a distraction now so go by instinct and seek out solitude when you feel like it.

AQUARIUS

FRIDAY, 8TH JANUARY
Moon trine Venus

You could have a rather nice day in company with in-laws or some other relative of your partner's today. A woman who is vaguely attached to you in this kind of way, will turn out to be amusing and interesting company. This person could help you work out how best to go about decorating or changing part of your home or, if you need some help from an experienced cook, she could be the one to come up with the right recipe.

SATURDAY, 9TH JANUARY
Moon square Sun

There's a touch of over sensitivity about you today. I know you can usually brazen out unpleasant encounters, but just at the moment, you'd far rather completely avoid awkward situations and people. Actually this is a good thing at the moment, so don't try to force yourself into any actions that you aren't completely happy with. Being assertive could hurt your interests just now.

SUNDAY, 10TH JANUARY
Moon opposite Saturn

If you're off on your travels today then be prepared to put up with some delays and detours along the way. Nothing really can go exactly to plan at the moment since the stressful influence of Saturn is out to disrupt your well-ordered plans. Difficulties must be borne with patience now.

MONDAY, 11TH JANUARY
Moon square Uranus

It may be hard for your to keep your mind firmly on your work today because, while you are well aware that there is much to be done, your mood is rather rebellious and resentful.

TUESDAY, 12TH JANUARY
Venus sextile Pluto

Your creative and inventive talents are at a peak today, so get started on making something totally individual. You seem to have some kind of extra charisma now so, if you want to attract a new lover or if you are keen to keep the romance going in a current relationship, then go all out for what you want. Dress yourself nicely now and make the world take notice of your new-found glamour.

AQUARIUS

WEDNESDAY, 13TH JANUARY
Venus conjunct Uranus

If others think that you're nothing but a staid stick-in-the-mud, then the shock value you cause today will be worth every gasp. Watch for all the raised eyebrows as you emerge like a butterfly from a chrysalis. Venus has contacted unconventional Uranus which causes you to cast caution to the winds and display a verve and fashion sense that may be daring, but is certainly uniquely you! Go with your instincts and sense of style now.

THURSDAY, 14TH JANUARY
Sun sextile Jupiter

You may find something that you thought you had lost today, for instance you may put your hands in the pocket of an old coat only to discover some money or an odd earring that had gone missing earlier in the year.

FRIDAY, 15TH JANUARY
Sun square Mars

Take care when working around the home, the farm, the factory, office, hospital or anywhere else where there are tools. A moment's lack of attention could lead you to burn or to hurt yourself. Take care!

SATURDAY, 16TH JANUARY
Moon conjunct Mercury

Your imagination is very strong and possibly a little too heated today. The Moon unites with Mercury in your solar house of the subconscious bringing many dreams and fantasies to light. Though these are things that you'd usually be inclined to keep to yourself, you'll be surprised at how easily you can communicate them to someone who understands.

SUNDAY, 17TH JANUARY
New Moon

The world of romance is especially attractive on a day when your dreams and fantasies take over your life. The New Moon points the way to new emotional experiences in the future, but you mustn't cling to the past because of misplaced loyalty or guilt. Some people are leaving your life, but if you were honest you'd admit that they're no real loss. Follow your instincts now and your dreams may well come true.

AQUARIUS

MONDAY, 18TH JANUARY
Sun square Saturn

With the Sun occupying your horoscope area of privacy and psychological drives there've been considerable changes of opinion forming for the last couple of weeks. An outside event could force some of these issues into the light of day now with unpredictable results. You've got to have confidence in your own views now even if they're challenged. Stand your ground, because you are in the right even if others refuse to acknowledge the fact.

TUESDAY, 19TH JANUARY
Moon conjunct Venus

There are some wonderful opportunities around for you to improve your financial position now but there are some equally good opportunities for finding a real bargain or for buying something that is going to stand the test of time. Romantically speaking, this should be a really comfortable day in which you and your lover snuggle up on the sofa and make an early start on the evening's entertainments!

WEDNESDAY, 20TH JANUARY
Sun into Aquarius

The Sun moves into your own sign today bringing with it a lifting of your spirits and a gaining of confidence all round. Your birthday will soon be here and we hope that it will be a good one for you. You may see more of your family than is usual now and there should be some socializing and partying to look forward too. Music belongs to the realm of the Sun, so treat yourself to a musical treat soon.

THURSDAY, 21ST JANUARY
Mars opposite Saturn

It's not going to be an easy day if you want anything done in a hurry! Mars opposes Saturn showing that your impatience is at fever pitch but that the circumstances are such that you'll have to slow down rather than speed up. If travelling, expect hitches and delays.

FRIDAY, 22ND JANUARY
Sun conjunct Neptune

The sense of reality takes a severe knock today as the Sun combines with Neptune to take your feet off the ground and stimulate a capacity for wishful thinking. I'm not one to discourage optimism but keep your expectations within bounds. However, this influence should be good for those who are involved in creative pursuits. Musicians and photographers are particularly favoured.

AQUARIUS

SATURDAY, 23RD JANUARY
Mercury sextile Jupiter

Give your imagination free rein today for no matter how high flown or improbable your fantasies seem, they may be closer to practicality than you realize. Jupiter's aspect to Mercury gives you an uncanny ability to see past the petty details to the grand design beyond. Financially, you'll see the potential in a project that everyone else has missed.

SUNDAY, 24TH JANUARY
Mercury square Saturn

You'll probably feel quite frustrated by your own inability to express yourself clearly today. You've got some deeply held convictions coming to the surface but no matter how hard you try they aren't quite ready to see the light of day just yet. You might even feel stupid or clumsy, which is nonsense. The important thing is not to blame yourself for a momentary awkwardness that others may not have even noticed.

MONDAY, 25TH JANUARY
Moon square Uranus

A rebellious youngster could set the cat amongst the pigeons today. No matter what you decide to do a child, or at least someone younger than yourself is convinced that they know better. Sometimes you can't win by persuasion so you'll be tempted to lay down the law. This will turn out to be a domestic storm in a teacup.

TUESDAY, 26TH JANUARY
Mars into Scorpio

It's now time for drive, force and ambition as Mars enters the career area encouraging you to forge ahead with plans. You may feel you want to take a more independent course so this influence favours those who run their own businesses. You'll be very brash and forthright.

WEDNESDAY, 27TH JANUARY
Venus sextile Saturn

A romantic attachment could soon develop between yourself and someone who has a serious turn of mind and a precise mode of speech. Even if love doesn't enter the picture you can be sure that you will create a meaningful friendship.

THURSDAY, 28TH JANUARY
Venus into Pisces

Your financial state should experience a welcome boost for a few weeks as Venus, one of the planetary indicators of wealth, moves into your solar house of possessions and economic security from today. You feel that you deserve a lifestyle full of luxury now and that'll be reflected in the good taste you express when making purchases for your home. Your sense of self-worth is boosted too which might indicate a renewed interest in high fashion.

FRIDAY, 29TH JANUARY
Venus trine Mars

With a combination of luck supplied by Venus, and a readiness to take urgent action courtesy of Mars, the heavens decree a day of good fortune both for your financial security and in the career stakes. There's a chance to apply for a better position or to shoulder more responsibility. Of course there will be an adequate recompense for any work you take on now. Don't dither today… act!

SATURDAY, 30TH JANUARY
Sun sextile Pluto

You look as though you're in for a pretty intense encounter today. A deep and soulful mood has gripped a friend and you're the one who has to deal with it. Fortunately, you have the ability to lift your friend's spirits.

SUNDAY, 31ST JANUARY
Full Moon eclipse

Today's eclipse casts a shadow of doubt over a close relationship. Problems that have been simmering under the surface will now come out and have to be faced. It's no good shying away from serious issues as this could be a make or break time.

February at a Glance

LOVE	❤	❤	❤		
WORK	★	★	★	★	
MONEY	£	£	£	£	£
HEALTH	✚	✚	✚	✚	
LUCK	♘	♘	♘	♘	♘

AQUARIUS

MONDAY, 1ST FEBRUARY
Mars square Neptune

There's a lot going on in your working world at the moment and, a lot is expected of you. However, you won't really be in the mood to tackle anything too arduous today. Even so, you can't afford to slacken off with so much attention on your performance.

TUESDAY, 2ND FEBRUARY
Sun conjunct Uranus

An independent and rebellious mood seizes you today as the Sun meets up with Uranus in your solar house of personality. You don't want to be hemmed in or held to any promises that you've rashly made. If those around you are wise, they'll give you the space you so desperately need now. Your restlessness in company is such that you'll be very irritable if friends and family are too demanding.

WEDNESDAY, 3RD FEBRUARY
Sun conjunct Mercury

Mercury and the Sun are in conjunction in your own sign today. This will bring success on many different fronts for you. Mercury is especially effective in regard to any form of communications. Therefore, if you need to get on the phone and to deal with things, you will make excellent progress today. It is a good day for starting projects, finding work or writing of any kind, so get going on that novel you have been thinking of for so long!

THURSDAY, 4TH FEBRUARY
Moon opposite Jupiter

There's no point in making any far-reaching decisions in partnership or financial affairs today. You're too scatterbrained to make any sensible choices so just go with the flow. Don't allow blind optimism to get in the way of reason now.

FRIDAY, 5TH FEBRUARY
Mercury conjunct Uranus

New concepts are hitting your brain at a tremendous pace today. I hope you aren't the shockable sort because some of them will be so way-out as to be completely mind-boggling. At least you've got the capacity to take a lot in, and come out with a few yourself. Who knows, this mental whirlwind could set you off on an entirely new direction. A great one for original thinking.

AQUARIUS

SATURDAY, 6TH FEBRUARY
Venus square Pluto

Are you positive that you know what you're doing economically? Are you also sure that other people are telling you the truth where money is concerned? Guard against predatory females because they could take more from you than you bargain for. If someone is pressuring you to sign on the dotted line you should dig in your heels and insist on reading the small print very carefully.

SUNDAY, 7TH FEBRUARY
Moon conjunct Mars

You may find yourself fighting with bureaucrats, officious officials, paranoid plutocrats or a parking-meter attendant. There is only so far you can get with this but there is no need for you to be pushed around. Perhaps a strongly worded letter to the right place will do the trick in straightening things out for you now.

MONDAY, 8TH FEBRUARY
Moon square Sun

There could be some kind of power struggle going on today. In practical terms, this could bring you up against an authority figure or someone who thinks rather a lot of themselves. This could also make things difficult for any business dealings that you have on the go at the moment. However, on a less practical note, you may doubt your own judgement for a while.

TUESDAY, 9TH FEBRUARY
Moon trine Jupiter

You have every reason in the world to be confident and outgoing today. The Moon's aspect to Jupiter makes you one of the most optimistic and popular people around. Financially, good news is on its way. I'm not promising anything spectacular but you'll still be smiling. If you want to take full advantage of today's stars then work out an investment plan with someone who knows the best policy.

WEDNESDAY, 10TH FEBRUARY
Moon sextile Uranus

It's time to put your work worries in their place and be social for once. You may have been neglecting the lighter, more pleasurable side of life so now's your chance to put that right. Your friends have been wondering what's happened to you, so pop around and satisfy their justifiable curiosity.

AQUARIUS

THURSDAY, 11TH FEBRUARY
Mercury sextile Saturn

If you are studying something or putting in any kind of mental effort you will soon start to see the results of this. You may have to teach or train others today and, if so, this will go well too. You may need to confer with an older person or someone who is in a position of responsibility today and they will take your ideas on board while, also giving you the credit for them.

FRIDAY, 12TH FEBRUARY
Mercury into Pisces

All the planets seem to be restless just now since Mercury changes sign today. At least you can get your mind into gear concerning the state of your finances now. Tasks you've been putting off like cancelling useless standing orders, or ensuring you receive the most advantageous interest from your savings will be tackled with ease now.

SATURDAY, 13TH FEBRUARY
Jupiter into Aries

Jupiter moves into its least happy position today, as it enters your Solar third house. Here the exuberance and optimism of the giant planet is somewhat muted by a tendency not to see other people's points of view. Your mind will be very active, but even though you'll easily accumulate facts you may not be able to put the lessons of life to their best use.

SUNDAY, 14TH FEBRUARY
Moon sextile Jupiter

St Valentine's Day should be quite pleasant and there may even be a bit of extra money in the offing for you. You may hear from a friend or a relative who is at a distance from you or you may find yourself on a pleasant journey now.

MONDAY, 15TH FEBRUARY
Moon conjunct Uranus

You will have to be prepared to adapt yourself to a number of new situations today because just about anything could be flung at you now. Life will be hectic, and not always easy to deal with or even to understand at times. Your mind will be buzzing with a number of ingenious ideas but they could be too far 'off the wall' to be truly practicable. You could hear some strange news via an older female member of the family.

TUESDAY, 16TH FEBRUARY
New Moon eclipse

It's a new start for you as the Solar Eclipse occurs in your sign. Put the past behind you. Close the door on all those things that have held you back. Painful memories might not actually go away, but at least you can put them in the perspective of your life as it is now. And indeed, as it will be in the future. Be positive, optimistic and outgoing. Its up to you to choose your future agenda now!

WEDNESDAY, 17TH FEBRUARY
Sun sextile Saturn

An older friend or relative may get in touch with you today. Alternatively, you could hear something good from a superior at your work. There is plenty of news coming your way today, some of it quite serious but all of it very positive and well worth hearing. You may be given an opportunity to speak up and to air your own personal opinion to those who matter.

THURSDAY, 18TH FEBRUARY
Mercury square Pluto

Though you may like to think that you lead your particular group with charm and persuasion, you will find that your increasingly tyrannical approach is rapidly turning one-time friends against you. Try to moderate your demands.

FRIDAY, 19TH FEBRUARY
Sun into Pisces

Your financial prospects take an upturn from today as the Sun enters your house of money and possessions. The next month should see an improvement in your economic security. It may be that you need to lay plans to ensure maximum profit now. Don't expect any swift returns from investments but lay down a pattern for future growth. Sensible monetary decisions made now will pay off in a big way.

SATURDAY, 20TH FEBRUARY
Void Moon

This is one of those days when none of the planets is making any worthwhile kind of aspect to any of the others. Even the Moon is 'void of course', which means that it is not making any aspects of any importance to any of the other planets. On such a day, avoid starting anything new and don't set out to do anything important. Do what needs to be done and take some time off for a rest.

AQUARIUS

SUNDAY, 21ST FEBRUARY
Venus into Aries

If you've got any favours to ask, the passage of Venus into your solar house of persuasion shows that you can use considerable charm and eloquence to win others over to your point of view with little trouble at all. A little flirtation combined with a winning way ensures that you achieve your desires. Your creative talents are boosted too so perhaps you should consider writing down your inspirations now.

MONDAY, 22ND FEBRUARY
Venus sextile Neptune

There's more than a touch of diplomacy and charm about you today. The splendid aspect between Venus and Neptune enables you to pour oil on troubled waters, calm down the hot feelings of others and generally chart a smooth course through life's complications with ease. You are also something of a culture vulture today since you'll be keen to enter the world of the arts in some way. You may not think of yourself as the creative type but give it a go, you could surprise yourself.

TUESDAY, 23RD FEBRUARY
Moon opposite Pluto

Though you are happy with the way your life is going at the moment, you may feel that there's an undercurrent of disapproval among your friends. Perhaps a new romance is causing your established friends to feel somewhat ignored. If that's not the case, then your anxieties concerning a friend could be quite obsessive. Calm yourself because there's very little you can do at present.

WEDNESDAY, 24TH FEBRUARY
Venus conjunct Jupiter

You may have a simply stupendous money-making idea today and the stars suggest that, if you tried to put this into action, it would work very well for you. This is certainly a great day to take on any kind of tricky negotiating or for signing important documents. You can use this ploy very successfully in personal relationships now, simply by negotiating with your loved ones for a better share of what you think you need.

THURSDAY, 25TH FEBRUARY
Moon trine Sun

This should be a day of harmony since the Sun and Moon are in perfect agreement. Your emotions will be under control so there's little that could upset you or cause any panic. Routine will be important to you now so you can organize your time to achieve the maximum benefit. Work, health and money matters are all favoured.

FRIDAY, 26TH FEBRUARY
Sun trine Mars

Your hard work has not gone unnoticed and will now be rewarded. The golden glow of the sun could bring a golden pay packet if you are extra lucky, and there's no reason why you shouldn't be.

SATURDAY, 27TH FEBRUARY
Jupiter sextile Neptune

International links and long-distance phone calls are the order of the day as Jupiter and Neptune get together to ensure a day of communication and excitement. You'll be chattering away happily and proving that your enthusiasm and good humour are infectious.

SUNDAY, 28TH FEBRUARY
Moon opposite Uranus

Any relationship difficulties you're experiencing at the moment are basically down to you. That's the message of the Lunar opposition to Uranus today. You're charting a ruggedly individualistic course without taking the feelings of your partner in life into consideration at all. Perhaps you haven't noticed that you're being selfish but that's no excuse. A gesture of affection now will successfully get you out of the doghouse.

March at a Glance

LOVE	❤	❤	❤		
WORK	★	★	★		
MONEY	£	£	£		
HEALTH	✚	✚	✚		
LUCK	⊍	⊍			

AQUARIUS

MONDAY, 1ST MARCH
Saturn into Taurus

You are just about to embark on a long drawn-out project in connection with property or premises. This may involve mortgages or calling in the builders to add extensions to what you already have. You may feel tied to a particular area over the next couple of years, but the outcome of all this effort and expense will be worthwhile.

TUESDAY, 2ND MARCH
Mercury into Aries

Your mind will be going at full speed ahead over the next few weeks and you are bound to come up with some really great new ideas. You will be very busy with the phone ringing off its hook and letters falling into your letter box by the ton. You will find yourself acting as a temporary secretary for a while, even if the only person who makes use of your services is yourself.

WEDNESDAY, 3RD MARCH
Venus trine Pluto

You shouldn't take anything for granted when Venus aspects Pluto. In affairs of the heart, a good talk will allow you to compare notes concerning your desires and aspirations. You may find that a friend who has been a pillar of strength in the past is no longer so apparent as a feature of your life. This needn't be a permanent situation, so though you may be slightly hurt you should remember that your friend has a life and problems to cope with of his or her own.

THURSDAY, 4TH MARCH
Venus sextile Uranus

There's a strong attraction to the unusual today. People you encounter who are somehow out of the ordinary will exert a powerful appeal. If you are extra lucky, the lure of romance will soon follow.

FRIDAY, 5TH MARCH
Mercury sextile Neptune

Your practical view of life will be of great help to someone around you who is in need at the moment. The cerebral planet Mercury gives a swift grasp of problems while Neptune brings a deep compassion and willingness to render assistance. You may have to work your way through difficult forms and documents for someone who hasn't got a clue. You're definitely the one for the job.

SATURDAY, 6TH MARCH
Moon square Neptune

Someone may try to undermine your position at work today. They may want to take the credit for what you have done in the past or they may want to make you look an incompetent fool. They seem to be jealous and unsure of themselves.

SUNDAY, 7TH MARCH
Moon square Uranus

You aren't a fan of being nagged by people who think they know best even when it's perfectly obvious that they don't. You aren't in the mood to be dictated to just now so anyone who tries will be in for a rude awakening. If you have some opposition to established authority, don't put yourself out on a limb before you ensure that you've got sufficient backing to get your own way.

MONDAY, 8TH MARCH
Moon trine Venus

A chat with a woman friend may be just the thing to help you get things into perspective today. You seem to need some kind of practical advice in order to prevent you from taking a rather foolish course of action. A pal may suggest an unexpected and rather unusual outing later in the day and you would be missing a lot of fun if you turn this down.

TUESDAY, 9TH MARCH
Moon trine Jupiter

Friends will want to talk over some of their problems today and you will be happy to lend a listening ear. You may feel like off-loading some of your worries on them too and the whole exercise will help you to put things into perspective again. This is also a rather lucky day for money and a gamble may pay off now too.

WEDNESDAY, 10TH MARCH
Mercury retrograde

Whenever Mercury moves into retrograde motion, you can expect a short period of muddles and misunderstandings. This is not a good time in which to try to sort out arguments or differences in business if you can avoid it. Leave everyone to simmer down for a while and, if the situation still needs a few words in two or three week's time, have a go at it then.

THURSDAY, 11TH MARCH
Moon square Mercury

I just knew all that talking was a mixed blessing. Your mind is racing so fast you can't help causing misunderstandings just now. You may also receive some wounding criticism, though you must admit that you're being a touch over-sensitive. If these hurtful words were actually meant to be constructive then you could do worse than thinking hard about the issues they raise.

FRIDAY, 12TH MARCH
Moon sextile Mars

Though you tend to be a forthright person, you must realize that going at problems like a bull at a gate isn't always the answer. Some tact and subtlety is required if you're going to get your own way now. Pay attention to the finer feelings of those around you, and they'll again allow you to take the lead.

SATURDAY, 13TH MARCH
Mercury sextile Neptune

Your practical view of life will be of great help to someone around you who is in need at the moment. The cerebral planet Mercury gives a swift grasp of problems while Neptune brings a deep compassion and willingness to render assistance. You may have to work your way through difficult forms and documents for someone who hasn't got a clue. You're definitely the one for the job.

SUNDAY, 14TH MARCH
Moon sextile Pluto

A reassessment of priorities is the order of the day. You've become aware of so many new possibilities in your life that it's time to ditch some old preconceptions and ambitions that have become irrelevant. You've got no time for those who want to live in the past or who can't see that the world has changed. These people may be drifting away and that has to be accepted too.

MONDAY, 15TH MARCH
Moon sextile Venus

Anyone who wishes to provoke you by starting on a controversial subject will be surprised when you retreat in panic. Serious topics are the last thing you want to tackle today. In fact, you'd prefer a conversation based on more mundane matters. You need a good laugh so some wit and gossip would be appreciated. Steer clear of anything too heavy.

TUESDAY, 16TH MARCH
Moon square Pluto

The lunar aspect to Pluto is a little alarming for your bank balance today. You'd be well advised to look over the facts and figures because there's been an error made somewhere and you can't afford to ignore it. At least you can get to the bottom of this little mystery but until you do you won't get much peace. In dealings with friends, tact and subtlety are important if you don't want to hurt their feelings.

WEDNESDAY, 17TH MARCH
New Moon

Today's New Moon shows that your financial affairs have reached a point where you have to make a decision. Do you carry on in the old, and rather dreary ways of making and spending your cash or will you look at the realities and make sensible decisions? This isn't a time to retreat into dreamland, or to carry on with bad budgeting. Look at your monetary state carefully now.

THURSDAY, 18TH MARCH
Venus into Taurus

Old scores and family squabbles can now be laid to rest as the passage of Venus into your domestic area signals a time of harmony and contentment. Surround yourself with beauty, both in terms of affection and in material possessions. This is a good time to renew a closeness with those you love. Join forces to complete a major project such as redecoration, or even a move of home itself. Be assured that the stars smile on you now.

FRIDAY, 19TH MARCH
Sun conjunct Mercury

This is an excellent day in which to pull of a really spectacular deal so, if you feel like wheeling and dealing in the big leagues, then do so today! Even if you are only looking around for something for yourself or your family, you should be able to find just what you want now. This is also a good time for buying or selling a vehicle, or for getting one put back into good working order.

SATURDAY, 20TH MARCH
Venus conjunct Saturn

Venus and Saturn are planets whose characteristics are very different from each other so it is hard to work out whether today's conjunction is likely to be a pleasant occasion or not. Anything that does arise from this planetary aspect will affect your family and domestic situation.

SUNDAY, 21ST MARCH
Sun into Aries

Your curiosity will be massively stimulated from today as the Sun enters the area of learning and communication. Other people's business suddenly becomes your own now. That's not to say that you turn into a busybody overnight, it's just that many will turn to you for some guidance. Affairs in the lives of your brothers, sisters and neighbours have extra importance now. Short journeys too are well starred for one month.

MONDAY, 22ND MARCH
Moon trine Neptune

The events of the day will prove that a lot of those things that you've taken for granted, perhaps for years are falling away from you now. The Moon's aspect to Neptune encourages you to trust to your instincts and follow a course that isn't totally reliant on observable facts. This is particularly true of all creative ventures and in the area of romance. An infatuation is on the cards for many.

TUESDAY, 23RD MARCH
Venus square Neptune

The contrary aspect between Venus and Neptune puts you in a dreamy frame of mind just when rapid action is required. The more pressure that's exerted upon you the more you'll be inclined to wrap yourself into a little ball and wish the world would go away. Of course, you'll develop a guilt complex along the way, but try to resist this negative urge. Perhaps you need some time to your own thoughts and dreams, and there's really very little that can't be put off if you really can't be bothered now.

WEDNESDAY, 24TH MARCH
Moon square Sun

You are going to spend a lot of time on the phone over the next month or so and you will also have a pile of correspondence to deal with. This may be the time in which you get to grips with a new computer program or some other kind of new technology. The age of the horse and cart, and also of the quill pen are over for you now, and you must get with it in order to cope with the modern world.

THURSDAY, 25TH MARCH
Sun sextile Neptune

Your mind has been on a practical course for some time now so today's aspect between the Sun and dreamy Neptune should make a refreshing change. This is your chance to show that there is a more spiritual side to your character and you're as susceptible to art and music as anyone else. You show a deep compassion now and your acts of kindness will win expressions of heartfelt gratitude. Some good news is on its way, which though it doesn't affect you directly will be very satisfying all the same.

AQUARIUS

FRIDAY, 26TH MARCH
Moon square Saturn

Sobering up can be an unpleasant experience especially when you are dragged away from something you enjoy to deal with a domestic crisis. It's obvious that you'll be the one who has to take control and calm down everyone around you. Of course, this is probably nothing more than a mountain made out of a molehill, but still it can't be left to the over-reactions of your family.

SATURDAY, 27TH MARCH
Venus opposite Mars

You may feel yourself held back and restricted by family opposition today. You'll know perfectly well what the right course to take is, but those around you will try to dissuade you from this.

SUNDAY, 28TH MARCH
Void Moon

Occasionally one finds a day in which neither the planets nor the Moon make any major aspects to each other and on such a day the Moon's course is said to be void. There is nothing wrong with a day like this but there is no point in trying to start anything new or anything important because there isn't enough of a planetary boost to get it off the ground. Stick to your normal routine.

MONDAY, 29TH MARCH
Moon square Pluto

The odd actions and evasive ways of a friend could start up your suspicions today. If there is a money matter involved in this then you have every right to be dubious. Make some subtle enquiries to find out exactly what's going on.

TUESDAY, 30TH MARCH
Jupiter trine Pluto

This is your chance to show off your leadership qualities, but take care that this doesn't turn you into a petulant tyrant. You will tend to dominate colleagues and friends at the moment, but someone has to get things organized, so why not you?

WEDNESDAY, 31ST MARCH
Full Moon

You may have to face the fact that you cannot slope off to distant and romantic shores just now. This doesn't mean that you are forever confined to your home, just that you cannot get away right now. Your mood is not only escapist but also rebellious today! You won't want to have anything to do with people who restrict you or who remind you of your chores and duties but you simply won't be able to escape them.

April at a Glance

LOVE	❤	❤	❤	❤
WORK	★	★		
MONEY	£	£	£	
HEALTH	✚	✚	✚	
LUCK	∪	∪	∪	∪

THURSDAY, 1ST APRIL
Sun conjunct Jupiter

There is good news about a number of things on the way to you now. There may be something positive happening in connection with a legal matter today, or possibly money coming in from something to do with contracts or documents. You may receive a tax rebate or an insurance payment today. New opportunities will arise and useful new contacts can be made now.

FRIDAY, 2ND APRIL
Mercury direct

The wayward planet Mercury resumes a direct motion today which will restore some order from the chaos that has beset your economic interests. Don't expect instant miracles though. The mass of paperwork and financial complication that has piled up while your attention was diverted will take some sorting out. At least now you're in a positive frame of mind and capable of handling the most vexed monetary questions with relative ease.

SATURDAY, 3RD APRIL
Moon conjunct Mars

Your career prospects receive a welcome boost as the Moon conjuncts Mars today. You're endowed with a tremendous energy that ensures success in whatever you do. You won't be inclined to suffer fools gladly now, and lazy people will get the sharp edge of your tongue because you can't see any reason why you should carry a burden for anyone else. Of course, with any Mars aspect there is the danger of wasted effort through haste, so remember to think before you act even if you are a dynamo.

SUNDAY, 4TH APRIL
Mercury sextile Venus

For once, you can have a sensible conversation about money and values with certain family members who have not, in the recent past, been too co-operative. Diplomatically, you can lay down ground rules that will be followed. It's all a matter of approach.

MONDAY, 5TH APRIL
Moon sextile Neptune

The finer side to your nature is perfectly expressed today. Your convictions and deeply held beliefs will be perfectly expressed by word and example. Charitable feelings are stirred and you'll be prepared to contribute time or cash to a worthy cause. Music and poetry are eloquent sustenance to your soul.

TUESDAY, 6TH APRIL
Saturn square Neptune

Long-established traditions are all well and good as long as they don't stifle future prospects. You may feel that carrying on an old custom has no relevance to the way you live your life now. However, abandoning it just like that could cause friction between yourself and older members of the family.

WEDNESDAY, 7TH APRIL
Sun sextile Uranus

Anyone in a position of authority is due for a shock today since you are in a rebellious frame of mind. You won't be willing to put up with foolish notions from those higher up the establishment structure so you'll be all too prepared to make your feelings known. In fact, you'll be impatient with any form of restriction especially those that are based on whims or outmoded practices in the workplace.

THURSDAY, 8TH APRIL
Moon sextile Mars

There are subtle forces working behind closed doors in the workplace, and it's about time you were aware of them. Decisions made now will have a great influence on you but it would be difficult to take all their consequences on board immediately. You can't change the intrigues in the corridors of power but with a little soft soap to those who matter you could get a better idea of what's going on.

AQUARIUS

FRIDAY, 9TH APRIL
Moon sextile Mercury

Keep a few matters to yourself today. Even if a friend or a neighbour tries to worm things out of you, try to keep your mouth firmly shut. Your financial position is improving rapidly now but it would be a good idea to keep this information to yourself just at the moment because there are plenty of people around you who would be only too happy to relieve you of any extra pennies that you may have put by.

SATURDAY, 10TH APRIL
Moon square Saturn

Home life doesn't seem to be the perfect garden of tranquillity that it should be for your psychological well-being at the moment. A dispute with a family member could sour the atmosphere for everybody if you let it. Get problems out in the open at once otherwise you'll be storing up resentment for the future.

SUNDAY, 11TH APRIL
Moon sextile Sun

This is a harmonious time when you can express the inner you and find warmth and understanding from those around you. You are charming and persuasive and will be showing your character off to the best advantage.

MONDAY, 12TH APRIL
Venus into Gemini

This is a good day to begin new projects and to get great ideas off the ground. Venus is now moving into the area of your chart that is concerned with creativity, so over the next few weeks you can take advantage of this and get involved with some kind of creative process. Venus is concerned with the production of beauty, so utilize this planetary energy to enhance any of your creations now.

TUESDAY, 13TH APRIL
Moon sextile Venus

A woman will prove to be very helpful to you now. She may help you to sort out a domestic problem and she could suggest ways that you save money too. If you need to employ someone to help in or around the house, the right person will come to the fore today. There are bargains to be had at the shops now, so get out and have a look around while the opportunity is there for you.

WEDNESDAY, 14TH APRIL
Moon into Aries

This is a tremendously exciting day as visitors drop in, the phone doesn't stop ringing and the whole world seems desperate for your company. Casual conversations could provide solutions to problems you thought were going to be with you forever. A brother or sister you haven't seen in ages may well get in touch.

THURSDAY, 15TH APRIL
Moon conjunct Jupiter

The phone or the post will bring some kind of unexpected opportunity your way today. This may bring an opportunity to join your friends and neighbours in a local event such as a Masonic Ladies Night or some other kind of regional or local celebration. There may be good news for brothers and sisters and they may pass some of their good fortune along to you if you are lucky.

FRIDAY, 16TH APRIL
New Moon

The New Moon shows a change in your way of thinking. In many ways you'll know that its time to move on. Perhaps you'll find yourself in a new company, a new home or among a new circle of friends in the near future. Opinions are set to change as you are influenced by more stimulating people. Perhaps you'll consider taking up an educational course of some kind.

SATURDAY, 17TH APRIL
Mercury into Aries

Your life is going to be extremely busy for a while now and there will be little time to sit around and rest. You will have more to do with friends, relatives, colleagues and neighbours than is usual and you could spend quite a bit of time sorting out minor domestic and work problems with workmen and women of various kinds. You may also spend time and money sorting out a vehicle.

SUNDAY, 18TH APRIL
Moon conjunct Venus

This should be a fun-packed day. The Moon and Venus get together in the most pleasurable area of your chart surrounding you with friendly faces and a lot of laughs. Female companionship is particularly stimulating and will increase your self-confidence and belief in your talents. For the romantically inclined, attractions of a physical nature abound.

AQUARIUS

MONDAY, 19TH APRIL
Mars opposite Saturn

Your patience could be sorely stretched today because everyone around you is very demanding. Both at work and in the domestic area, people want you to be in two places at once, doing at least three things and probably juggling as well! Try to keep a rein on your temper!

TUESDAY, 20TH APRIL
Sun into Taurus

The home and family become your main interest over the next four weeks as the Sun moves into the most domestic area of your chart from today. Family feuds will now be resolved, and you'll find an increasing contentment in your own surroundings. A haven of peace will be restored in your home. This should also be a period of nostalgia when happy memories come flooding back.

WEDNESDAY, 21ST APRIL
Venus opposite Pluto

You may find it hard to relate to people who are much older or much younger than you are today. The generation gap seems to be alive and well among your friends and your family at the moment. Don't try pressing your point of view on them just now.

THURSDAY, 22ND APRIL
Mercury sextile Neptune

You have a poetic soul, and this will be expressed in the most charming way today. The mingled influences of Neptune and Mercury will give you the ability to verbally express yourself in the right way and at the right time. Some will be amazed by your depth of understanding.

FRIDAY, 23RD APRIL
Jupiter sextile Uranus

Anyone who thought that they knew you inside out will have a shock today! You will be unexpectedly jovial, with a sudden enthusiasm for something totally new. This change of pace could rock others on their heels, yet your exuberant optimism will soon win them over!

SATURDAY, 24TH APRIL
Sun opposite Mars

Don't be too trusting today because someone is trying to pry into your private business. Even if all your affairs are above board, it still is an infringement of your rights. Before you allow your temper to get the better of you, wouldn't it be wise to find out exactly why this subtle investigation is going on? Then, and only then, can you take direct and decisive action.

SUNDAY, 25TH APRIL
Moon trine Saturn

It's a difficult day but one that has to be faced if you're to put old irritations behind you once and for all. Some duties have to be faced and you can't put these off any longer. The best advice is to get your head down and race through them as quickly as possible. That way, the painful experience will be over as soon as possible. Difficult forms and documents will be a major part in all this, so pay attention to the small print.

MONDAY, 26TH APRIL
Mercury trine Pluto

The picture is now clearing as you see what needs to be done to put your life on course. You have many unfulfilled ambitions, but it doesn't have to stay that way. The link between Mercury and Pluto will show you the path to greater fulfilment.

TUESDAY, 27TH APRIL
Sun conjunct Saturn

The Sun's conjunction with the sober planet Saturn concentrates your mind wonderfully. You now realize that many of your worries and concerns were trivial and you'll be determined to get to grips with the basic issues. In home life especially the accent is on hard work for long-term results. It'll be obvious to family members that you aren't to be disturbed for anything less than matters of earth-shattering importance.

WEDNESDAY, 28TH APRIL
Moon opposite Mercury

Watch your words today, because as quickly as you open your mouth, you'll manage to offend somebody. You may not mean to be sarcastic or indiscreet but for some reason your brain isn't tied into your speech centres at the moment. At the very least you'll be talking at cross-purposes with someone today. At worst, you'll turn a friend into an enemy by blurting out a private confidence that shouldn't be spoken.

THURSDAY, 29TH APRIL
Mercury sextile Uranus

There's an element of genius about you today. The two planets of mentality,

Mercury and Uranus, are in excellent aspect ensuring an inspiring and creative outlook. Your personality will shine as innovative thoughts become apparent to all. Originality is the key to success. Dare to be different!

FRIDAY, 30TH APRIL
Full Moon

Today's Full Moon shows that important decisions have to be made at a time of rapidly changing circumstances. News that arrives today could well be disturbing yet will prove to be a blessing in disguise in the long run. You may be considering a move of home, possibly to a distant location. Or even throwing in your present career to take up an educational course of some kind. People you meet while travelling will have important words to say.

May at a Glance

LOVE	❤				
WORK	★	★	★	★	★
MONEY	£	£	£	£	£
HEALTH	✚	✚			
LUCK	⊍	⊍	⊍		

SATURDAY, 1ST MAY
Mercury conjunct Jupiter

Today is a better day for travel or for making travel arrangements and this goes for local journeys as well as long-distance ones. Nevertheless, it would be worth taking the precaution of paying a bit more in order to get tickets that can be changed or refunded if necessary. This is also a pretty good day for dealing with business or money matters or for signing important papers.

SUNDAY, 2ND MAY
Moon sextile Neptune

You'll be in a very caring frame of mind today as your higher nature is stirred by the plight of those who are less fortunate than yourself. Your convictions will be superbly shown by your considerate words and actions. You will be someone to emulate today.

AQUARIUS

MONDAY, 3RD MAY
Moon sextile Uranus

Though you tend to prefer the tried and true, you won't lose out if you look for a short cut today. Try some lateral thinking because all is not as it seems now. A friend or colleague may be helpful in pointing you in the right direction now. Don't be afraid to try something new because its likely to be better than sticking to the old ways of doing things. Socially, you'll be attracted to a new venue.

TUESDAY, 4TH MAY
Moon opposite Venus

The chances are that a female friend could let you down today. She may not intend to do this, she may not be able to help herself. Those of you who are dating a potential lover may find that your plans to meet become fouled up and you wait for each other at the wrong place. Worse still, you may get off on the wrong foot with a new colleague at work.

WEDNESDAY, 5TH MAY
Mars into Libra

You could find yourself travelling over great distances at some time during the next few weeks. You may be asked to visit friends or family who live overseas now or you may simply take advantage of a good holiday offer. You may restrict your travelling to mental journeys by taking up a course of study or training now.

THURSDAY, 6TH MAY
Moon square Jupiter

Watch what you say today because it will come out wrong and you will cause misunderstandings all around. Don't sign anything important or agree to anything important now and don't buy any large or expensive items today. Travel is not particularly well starred today either.

FRIDAY, 7TH MAY
Neptune retrograde

The retrograde of Neptune which occurs today brings a confusing yet subtle influence into your life. You may feel less convinced of previously strongly held opinions and will be prepared to entertain more way-out notions. You'll have to take care that a strongly developed sense of compassion isn't taken advantage of by unscrupulous people. You should be too keen to make long-reaching decisions until Neptune returns to his proper course in October.

AQUARIUS

SATURDAY, 8TH MAY
Mercury into Taurus

The past exerts a powerful influence as Mercury enters the house of heritage. You'll find that things long forgotten will somehow re-enter your life over the next couple of weeks. An interest in your family heritage may develop, or possibly a new-found passion for antiques. Some good, meaningful conversations in the family will prove enlightening.

SUNDAY, 9TH MAY
Mercury sextile Venus

Your mind and your heart seem to be in harmony with each other today. Your family are on your side and nobody wants to upset you. All is sweetness and light at work too.

MONDAY, 10TH MAY
Moon square Pluto

Though a friend may come to you with a financial proposal that at first sight would put you into the high-income bracket, don't be too ready to fall in with a scheme that may be nothing more than pie in the sky. I know you won't want to pour cold water on any aspirations, but I doubt whether the sums will actually add up. Err on the side of caution in all monetary dealings today.

TUESDAY, 11TH MAY
Mercury square Neptune

If anyone expects you to sort out a family crisis today, they'd be well advised to leave you alone. You're so vague that you're likely to make the situation worse rather than solving it!

WEDNESDAY, 12TH MAY
Moon trine Pluto

A good talk with an old friend should go a long way to resolving some of the more puzzling things that have been happening to your recently. Even in a frivolous social setting you can develop a serious conversation with far-reaching intellectual concepts. Perhaps you'll be inclined to join a club or society that's concerned with the environment or political issues.

THURSDAY, 13TH MAY
Mercury conjunct Saturn

Precision is the key to success in all matters when Mercury conjuncts Saturn. Vague ideas are all very well in initial stages of any enterprise but NOW's the time to get down to the nitty-gritty of planning. It's obvious that you've got some big plans for your home so now you need to work out the best way to go about them. You've got no illusions about the amount of hard work to be done, but equally you know that you're up to it.

FRIDAY, 14TH MAY
Moon sextile Venus

They say that the good things in life are free, though you may have doubts on that score, you're convinced that life's not worth living unless you're enjoying yourself. The only trouble with that is that you'll be inclined to over-indulge today. Good food and wines are for gourmets, so make sure that you aren't a glutton!

SATURDAY, 15TH MAY
New Moon

The New Moon falls in the sphere of home and family today indicating a need for a change. For some reason you've been dissatisfied with your domestic set-up so you may consider looking at house prices in your own, or indeed another area. You probably feel that you need more space and light in your life that your present home isn't providing. A family member may be considering setting up home and deserves all the encouragement you can give.

SUNDAY, 16TH MAY
Venus sextile Saturn

An uncharacteristic aura of gloom descends as Venus and Saturn cast a chill over your working life. You may be affected by the negative vibes of those around you and could carry this despondent atmosphere home with you if you aren't careful. There's little scope to express yourself freely now since the weight of duty hangs heavy on your shoulders.

MONDAY, 17TH MAY
Mercury square Uranus

Disturbing news from a family member is on the agenda for today. However, don't over-react! Information you get now is likely to be totally inaccurate. Wait a while before you involve yourself!

TUESDAY, 18TH MAY
Moon sextile Saturn

Your parents may be able to help you out in some way today. Any dealings with older people or parental figures will go well now and they, themselves may have something to celebrate at this time.

AQUARIUS

WEDNESDAY, 19TH MAY
Moon square Jupiter

There may be trouble and uncertainty at your place of work and you may feel that you are doing far more than you are being paid for. Apart from that you probably won't be feeling at your best. Perhaps you are in one of those moods when you over-react to everything.

THURSDAY, 20TH MAY
Moon opposite Neptune

There's a lot of uncertainty around today especially in affairs of the heart. You want to know exactly where you stand but emotions by nature aren't going to yield up their complexities to analysis. A new relationship may seem too good to be true, but you can't work out whether you're being too cynical or not. Perhaps you're prone to suspicion now, if so try to cool down because it's hard to work anything out logically today.

FRIDAY, 21ST MAY
Sun into Gemini

You are going to be in a slightly frivolous frame of mind over the next few weeks and you shouldn't punish yourself for this. Pay attention to a creative interest or a demanding hobby now or get involved in something creative on behalf of others. A couple of typical examples would be to be the production of a school play or making preparations for a flower and vegetable show.

SATURDAY, 22ND MAY
Uranus retrograde

You are beginning to realize that you are projecting the wrong image right now. It is hard for others to trust you if you look eccentric or unreliable. Now is the time, therefore, to look as if your outlook is substantial, reliable and practical. There is no need to get too bogged down in plodding respectability or to turn your internal clock back to old-fashioned ways of thinking, it is just a matter of looking a bit more respectable for a while.

SUNDAY, 23RD MAY
Mercury into Gemini

Mercury moves into a part of your horoscope that is concerned with creativity. Mercury rules such things as thinking, learning and communications, but it can also be associated with skills and craftwork of various kinds. The combination of creativity and craftwork suggest that the next few weeks would be a good time to work on hobbies such as dressmaking, carpentry and so on.

AQUARIUS

MONDAY, 24TH MAY
Moon trine Mercury

There is a youthful atmosphere around you today, and this means that you could spend the day with younger members of your family or that you could help out at a school event of some kind. You will be amazed at the depth and openness of youngsters' minds and you could be quite inspired by their ideas. You may try your hand at a new sport or game now.

TUESDAY, 25TH MAY
Sun trine Neptune

You're certainly in a tender and affectionate mood as the Sun makes a splendid aspect to Neptune today. Anything brash and ugly will get short shrift as your mind is set on those things that lift the spirit and gladden the eye. Your taste is particularly refined now, and if you can share an artistic experience with someone of a like mind, your joy will be complete.

WEDNESDAY, 26TH MAY
Sun conjunct Mercury

Communication is the name of the game today as this will enhance all your relationships. You could have a really enjoyable chat to a friend or you could sit and talk things over with your lover today. You may decide to start a creative venture now and, if so, this is the time to do some research on your ideas and to see what materials and methods would best suit your purpose.

THURSDAY, 27TH MAY
Moon square Neptune

You seem to be doubting your own actions at the moment. You may not be sure that you are working towards the right goal and it may be necessary for you to make a change of direction soon. You appear keen to look for a lifestyle that means more to you than money alone.

FRIDAY, 28TH MAY
Moon square Uranus

Don't be stubborn today. There are setbacks and minor hold-ups in all areas at one time or another, but today the hassles seem concentrated in the career. If you can admit that you can make a mistake, and are willing to take advice then this needn't be a disaster. If, however you're determined to carry on regardless… you'll only have yourself to blame when it all goes wrong.

SATURDAY, 29TH MAY
Mars opposite Jupiter

Take care while travelling today. If you can avoid taking any kind journey now you would be doing yourself a favour. However, if you must travel, then allow extra time for delays, breakdowns and other frustrations.

SUNDAY, 30TH MAY
Full Moon

Today's Full Moon could make you feel a bit tetchy and tense and it could also bring you some sort of unexpected expense. The best thing to do today, is to stick to your usual routine and not start anything new or important. Jog along as usual and try not to become caught up in anybody else's bad mood now.

MONDAY, 31ST MAY
Venus square Mars

The daily habits of life seem all too restricting and limited at the moment and you'll be looking for something to alleviate your boredom. You know that there's more to life than the usual grind and will be anxious for new experience and stimulation. It's unfortunate that your self-expression suffers from this mood so try not to be too negative or sarcastic to those around you.

June at a Glance

LOVE	❤	❤	❤	❤	❤
WORK	★	★	★	★	★
MONEY	£	£	£	£	£
HEALTH	☉	☉	☉	☉	☉
LUCK	♘	♘	♘		

TUESDAY, 1ST JUNE
Venus square Jupiter

There is no escaping the fact that you have plenty of work to do just now and it is absolutely no good trying to ignore it. If you get what you have to do out of the way as quickly as possible today, there will still be some time for your pastimes and amusements later on.

AQUARIUS

WEDNESDAY, 2ND JUNE
Sun opposite Pluto

Someone around you is acting like a petty dictator, and for the sake of peace you've tended to put up with it. No matter what your personal feelings on the subject, this tyranny can't be tolerated any longer and you'll have to make a stand today just to retain your self-respect. It could be that this will be a clearing of the air. At least certain demarcation lines will be drawn and that's better for all concerned.

THURSDAY, 3RD JUNE
Mars direct

Mars resumes a direct course from today so all the hold-ups and difficulties you've experienced should now be over. When considering travel, all arrangements will now go smoothly. Of course Mars always promotes haste so I'd slow down if I were you and make up your mind about your choice of destination in a cooler frame of mind.

FRIDAY, 4TH JUNE
Mercury trine Mars

If ever there was a day for adventure this is it! Mercury combines with Mars inspiring you with a desire for freedom and excitement. An excellent outlook for travel, sporting ventures and foreign contacts.

SATURDAY, 5TH JUNE
Venus into Leo

Venus, the planet of romance moves into your horoscope area of close relationships from today increasing your physical desires and bringing the light of love into your heart. If you're involved in a long-term partnership it's a chance to renew the magic of the early days of your union. If single, then the next few weeks should bring a stunning new attraction into your life.

SUNDAY, 6TH JUNE
Moon square Pluto

A friend may try to convince you that he or she is a real financial wizard. Unfortunately it's all talk so don't be taken in by mistaken words of advice no matter how highly you regard their source. In some areas you need firmer, more sensible advice so idle chat isn't going to relieve your anxieties over your cash. If tempted to make an investment, check the figures once again to make sure that everything is above board.

AQUARIUS

MONDAY, 7TH JUNE
Mercury into Cancer

The movement of Mercury into your Solar sixth house of work, duties and health suggest that a slightly more serious phase is on the way. Over the next three weeks or so you will have to concentrate on what needs to be done rather than on having a good time. You may have a fair bit to do with neighbours, colleagues and relatives of around your own age group soon and you will have to spend a fair bit of time on the phone to them.

TUESDAY, 8TH JUNE
Sun trine Uranus

A day of pleasant surprises, especially when you consider affairs of the heart. A sudden meeting with someone destined to become emotionally important is forecast for many, while others will receive strong emotional support in an existing relationship.

WEDNESDAY, 9TH JUNE
Moon sextile Uranus

Don't stand there like a wallflower waiting to be introduced to all and sundry... it just won't work. Stop being so formal and make yourself known. Get into the swing of things and crack a few jokes. You'll soon find attention flatteringly turning your way.

THURSDAY, 10TH JUNE
Venus opposite Neptune

Fantasy mingles with fact to a most confusing extent today, since either you or a close partner can't disentangle a sad tale that doesn't exactly add up. Sympathies are stirred certainly, but you can't really be sure that your feelings aren't misplaced today. This is especially true if someone is trying some emotional blackmail to get their own way. It may be difficult but you should be firm now.

FRIDAY, 11TH JUNE
Moon square Uranus

There's something about your home that you don't like. Perhaps you're sick of looking at the same four walls all the time and are anxious to move out. If your dissatisfaction doesn't go that far you may think that its high time you redecorated. Don't do anything rash such as ripping paper off the walls just yet because your other half may have totally different ideas.

SATURDAY, 12TH JUNE
Moon trine Neptune

You're creatively inspired under the light of Neptune and the Moon today. Creative ventures will give you a sense of accomplishment and prove once and for all that you are unique. You need to relax your mind by doing something totally different from your usual duties. Try painting or music to lift your spirits. The romantically inclined shouldn't have any complaints because the stars make you receptive to proposals.

SUNDAY, 13TH JUNE
New Moon

There's a New Moon today casting a glow over your artistic potential. Your talents should shine now so have some belief in yourself and in what you can offer to the world at large. Of course if art and literature leave you cold, you may be more inclined to an amorous path. Conventional values are not for you now since you're determined to be yourself and to chart your own course. Make time to have fun, you deserve it.

MONDAY, 14TH JUNE
Venus trine Pluto

Today's Venusian aspect to Pluto could transform your love life. If you're attached, a social event could renew the sparkle to your partnership. If single, then a friend could be seen in a new and more romantic light. Your heart will rule your head in a delightful way.

TUESDAY, 15TH JUNE
Mercury sextile Saturn

You are becoming increasingly aware of the need to look after your health these days. Maybe this is the day that you give up smoking or perhaps you decide to take some more exercise from now on.

WEDNESDAY, 16TH JUNE
Sun trine Mars

It's going to be an action-packed day as the Sun and Mars make energetic contact. Romantic affairs flourish as you're in a passionate mood and ready for fun. More creatively, you'll be a whirlwind indulging yourself in any pleasurable pastime that takes your fancy. Travel also goes well on this exciting day. Of course you've got to be careful you don't wear yourself out. At the moment though you're having too much fun to care.

THURSDAY, 17TH JUNE
Moon opposite Uranus

Though you've got plenty of love in your heart for family, friends and of course your partner, there are some times when you just wish they'd all leave you alone. If you feel too restricted and hemmed in today, you're likely to react by being irritable and awkward. So, if those around you have any sense they'll give you some extra space right now.

FRIDAY, 18TH JUNE
Moon trine Jupiter

If you are offered an opportunity to work in partnership with someone else, then do have a look at this today. The work that is involved may be some kind of business but it could be a fund-raising project or helping with a local event. There is a sporty feeling to the day, so if you do enjoy any kind of sporting outlet, have a go at it today.

SATURDAY, 19TH JUNE
Venus square Saturn

Disruptions in your home and family leave you lost for words, but when bad feeling spills over into a close relationship it's time to call a halt. Confronting the matter won't solve much today so it's best to withdraw from the field of combat for a while to allow everyone to cool off a little. Harmony can be restored but everyone involved has to make an effort.

SUNDAY, 20TH JUNE
Sun sextile Jupiter

If you fancy taking a small gamble, then today is the day for it. Don't go mad and put your shirt on anything, the planets are not that spectacular! But a small wager should be fun and it should come up smelling of roses for you. You can be cheeky, childish and positively daft if you want to today, because this is a time to have fun and to be totally irresponsible for a change.

MONDAY, 21ST JUNE
Sun into Cancer

The Sun moves into your Solar sixth house of work and duty for the next month. This Solar movement will also encourage you to concentrate on your health and well-being and also that of your family. If you are off-colour, the Sun will help you to get back to full health once again. If you have jobs that need to be done, the next month or so will be a good time to get them done.

AQUARIUS

TUESDAY, 22ND JUNE
Venus opposite Uranus

Long-standing relationships are likely to be a minefield today. Venus, planet of love opposes eccentric Uranus, showing that literally anything can happen! If you thought that you knew your other half inside out, prepare to be amazed!

WEDNESDAY, 23RD JUNE
Mercury square Mars

Once you see your situation clearly, it's too easy to irritate you with hidebound attitudes and narrow-minded views. You are in the fortunate position for seeing the way forward without confusion or being distracted by irrelevancies, unfortunately those around you don't have the benefit of your keen perception. It would be best to patiently explain your intentions… if, that is, you can be bothered to spend time with those who are out of tune with your thoughts.

THURSDAY, 24TH JUNE
Moon opposite Saturn

Sometimes you feel hemmed in and far too restricted in your actions by those who don't understand your motivations or good qualities. You don't like miserable people at the best of times since you find that the mood seems to rub off. Unfortunately it's just one of those days when you encounter grim folk again and again. Keep smiling and don't take their negativity to heart.

FRIDAY, 25TH JUNE
Mercury square Jupiter

Your thinking may be muddled today and any decisions that you take could be quite wrong. Don't sign anything important and don't agree to anything where money or business is concerned. You are not in possession of the full facts and you will pay the price for any impetuosity that you display at this time. Take a cool, calm and long-term view of any business, financial or legal matters.

SATURDAY, 26TH JUNE
Mercury into Leo

The inquisitive Mercury moves into your Solar house of marriage and long-lasting relationships from today ushering in a period when a renewed understanding can be reached between yourself and your partner. New relationships can be formed under this influence too though these will tend to be on a light, fairly superficial level. Good humour and plenty of chat should be a feature for a few weeks, though you must try to curb a tendency to needlessly criticize another's foibles. Remember, not even you are perfect!

AQUARIUS

SUNDAY, 27TH JUNE
Moon trine Venus

Women friends will rally to your cause today and they will be only too happy to rush round and take you out of yourself. You may receive an unexpected compliment from an admirer and, more importantly perhaps, your boss could show you just how much he or she appreciates you today. It would be a good idea to go out for a drink and a meal with a woman friend later in the day.

MONDAY, 28TH JUNE
Jupiter into Taurus

Your innate kindness and compassion for others is being stimulated now by the entry of Jupiter in your Solar area of family, home and heritage. Your protective instincts will be strongly stimulated in the coming months. However, you may tend to be rather possessive without allowing loved ones the opportunity of standing on their own two feet.

TUESDAY, 29TH JUNE
Moon trine Saturn

You may be dreaming about the kind of home you would like to live in and, while it may not be possible to have what you want now, there does seem to be a chance that you will get it in the long run.

WEDNESDAY, 30TH JUNE
Mercury opposite Neptune

An opposition between Mercury, the planet of mentality, and Neptune, planet of dreams, will make it hard for you to concentrate fully on anything today. However despite this mental mist, you may well experience some very meaningful thoughts and dreams.

July at a Glance

LOVE	❤	❤	❤	❤	❤
WORK	★	★	★	★	★
MONEY	£	£	£	£	
HEALTH	✚	✚			
LUCK	∪	∪			

AQUARIUS

THURSDAY, 1ST JULY
Moon sextile Pluto

A reassessment of priorities is the order of the day. You've become aware of so many new possibilities in your life that it's time to ditch some old preconceptions and ambitions that have become irrelevant. You've got no time for those who want to live in the past or who can't see that the world has changed. These people may be drifting away and that has to be accepted too.

FRIDAY, 2ND JULY
Moon opposite Venus

Someone very close to you is feeling a terrible burden of insecurity now. It may be that some harsh facts recently faced have shaken confidence. Some reassurance from you is now vital. Remember that you too can be prone to over-sensitivity so have some sympathy with one who needs your presence now.

SATURDAY, 3RD JULY
Moon trine Mars

There should be great news about money today and the evidence is that this will come from the mainstream of your job rather than from an out-of-the-blue windfall. If you have had to budget in order to get out of money problems in the past, you will now begin to see that your actions have been right and that this is having the effect you were looking for.

SUNDAY, 4TH JULY
Mars opposite Jupiter

Luck is definitely not with you so, avoid taking chances today. Don't lend money to anyone, you won't see any of it back. Don't enter any kind of business or family arrangement that you aren't happy with and don't accept that invitation to go bungee jumping either!

MONDAY, 5TH JULY
Mars into Scorpio

The dynamic planet Mars moves into your Solar area of career and ambition from today adding considerable zest to your working life. Any confusions in this sphere will now be firmly dispelled, for the red planet is an indicator of action not thought! You want immediate results and won't put up with any delaying tactics as you cut through red tape to get to the top. Impatience though is a double-edged sword, though it gets results, you may also store up some resentment of your aggressive manner.

AQUARIUS

TUESDAY, 6TH JULY
Moon square Sun

It wouldn't be a good idea to overload your schedule too much today. I know that you're bounding with self-confidence but the vitality levels just aren't up to it at the moment. If you're working, the evening won't come around fast enough. If not, then leave domestic chores for now. A few unwashed dishes aren't the end of the world.

WEDNESDAY, 7TH JULY
Moon trine Venus

Social opportunities are all around you now, so don't sit around on your own when there are people out there who'd welcome your company. Pop into a neglected friend's for a cup of tea and a chat, you'll be glad you made the effort as well as cheering up someone who needs it. Pick up the phone and ring a distant friend or one or two of your relatives for a good old gossip today.

THURSDAY, 8TH JULY
Mercury trine Pluto

Though you may be prone to some dark, suspicious thoughts concerning your partner or friends, you also realize that some issues have to be aired. Brooding won't solve anything so speak up. You will find out where you stand and may solve any problems completely.

FRIDAY, 9TH JULY
Moon square Venus

A quiet, undemanding day is just what you need. Home comforts and the satisfaction of being surrounded by love shows you that life really is worth living. Take this time to relax and build yourself up for the week ahead. Your friends and family are likely to call in unexpectedly, so make sure you have enough bread, milk and anything else that they are likely to need in the cupboard.

SATURDAY, 10TH JULY
Moon sextile Mercury

It's time for fun and togetherness as the Moon and Mercury highlight romantic potentials and partnerships. Forget mundane worries and get out with the sole aim of enjoying yourself. The presence of someone special makes this a time to remember.

SUNDAY, 11TH JULY
Mars square Neptune

You could find yourself in the unpleasant situation of being blamed for someone else's mistakes today. A boss or person in authority won't want to listen to reason and will strike out at the first available target, namely you! However, you won't take this sort of treatment lying down!

MONDAY, 12TH JULY
Mercury retrograde

In all partnerships, both business and of a more personal nature, misunderstandings, cross-purposes and ill-timed words are likely as Mercury embarks on a retrograde course from today. The next few weeks should see a lot of confusion. You must be as clear as crystal in all you say, otherwise arguments will result simply because one or other will have caught the wrong end of the stick.

TUESDAY, 13TH JULY
New Moon

Today's New Moon gives you the stamina to shrug off any minor ailments that have been troubling you. Occurring, as it does, in your solar house of health and work, its obvious that you need to get yourself into shape to face the challenges that await you. A few early nights, a better diet and a readiness to give up bad habits such as smoking, will work wonders.

WEDNESDAY, 14TH JULY
Moon conjunct Mercury

Spend today in the company of someone you love. You need some emotional reassurance and can only get it by an affectionate heart-to-heart. The beginning of any sort of partnership, romantic or business is strongly favoured today.

THURSDAY, 15TH JULY
Venus trine Jupiter

You can afford to indulge yourself, either by enjoying a long, languid soak in a softly scented bubble bath or by treating yourself and your loved ones to a special meal and a great night out. This is a wonderful time for purchasing luxury items for the home as well. In short, forget that you are one of the world's workers for once, and live like a lord for a day!

FRIDAY, 16TH JULY
Mercury trine Pluto

A strange and fascinating person is set to enter your circle today. You will be captivated by the depth of perception and personal magnetism of this character. Who knows, this intellectual attraction may eventually turn into romance.

AQUARIUS

SATURDAY, 17TH JULY
Void Moon

The Moon is 'void of course' today, so don't bother with anything important and don't start anything new now. Stick to your usual routines and don't change your lifestyle in any way.

SUNDAY, 18TH JULY
Saturn square Uranus

Your family will provide more than the usual number of problems today. Dealing with parents, children and fraternal relatives will be more of a chore than anything else, especially when you'd far rather be doing other things.

MONDAY, 19TH JULY
Moon trine Uranus

Traditional ways of tackling things won't hold much appeal today. The Moon makes a marvellous aspect to Uranus inspiring you to take a look at the benefits that modern technology can bring to your life. Even if you've never had the slightest inclination to enter the world of computers, laser discs and hi-tech music centres, there's likely to be a sudden change in attitude when you see exactly what they can do, and the difference they could make to your lifestyle.

TUESDAY, 20TH JULY
Moon square Sun

Though you have the promise of high achievement coming up, its important that you don't overload your schedule or take on far more than you can comfortably cope with. It's very tempting to push hard now, but watch out for the law of diminishing returns. The more you take on, the more tired you'll be and the harder the effort needed to complete your tasks. Be easy on yourself. Everything is going well so coast along with it. You don't need to store up stressful problems for the future.

WEDNESDAY, 21ST JULY
Jupiter square Neptune

Unrealistic members of your family could easily get fired up by a totally daft scheme today. But try as you might you will not be able to inject any hint of common sense into their thinking.

THURSDAY, 22ND JULY
Mercury square Mars

So much to do and so little time at your disposal! That's the way you feel today as a mountain of tasks await your attention. Your partner too may be extra demanding and you simply have to make time to fit everything in. The advice is… Don't panic! You can get around everything with a little forethought. Organize your time sensibly.

FRIDAY, 23RD JULY
Sun into Leo

The Sun moves into the area of your chart devoted to relationships from today. If things have been difficult in a partnership, either personal or in business, then this is your chance to put everything back into it proper place. It's obvious that the significant other in your life deserves respect and affection and that's just what you're now prepared to give. Teamwork is the key to success over the next month.

SATURDAY, 24TH JULY
Moon sextile Uranus

If you feel that the pressures of work are getting too much for you, then today is the day to call a halt! Take a break from the boring routine and have some well-deserved fun. The world won't screech to a stop simply because you take some time off you know!

SUNDAY, 25TH JULY
Mercury square Jupiter

There seems to be a measure of disagreement around you over money matters today. Some members of your family may consider that others shouldn't be spending what they want to spend, or that they should be spending their money in a different way or on different things. You, yourself may be accused to being too profligate with the pennies (or cents, dollars or anything else that you can get your sticky little hands on!)

MONDAY, 26TH JULY
Sun opposite Neptune

You can't hope to get your point across when the Sun and Neptune are in such a confusing aspect. Someone close is living in a fantasy world and no matter how much you point out the flaws in his or her ideas you haven't a hope of dispelling the clouds of illusion. Misunderstandings and talking at cross-purposes are the features of the day but do make the attempt to be crystal clear in all you say.

TUESDAY, 27TH JULY
Sun square Jupiter

Oh boy, today is going to be an expensive one! Something is going to be more costly than you had bargained for and that 'affordable' luxury is likely to be a real drain on your resources. If this wasn't enough, your partner may take a dim view of this sudden development on your part of a desire to live like a millionaire. Try to avoid ending the day falling out over this.

WEDNESDAY, 28TH JULY
Full Moon eclipse

There is a full Moon eclipse in your own sign today and this will bring something sharply into focus for you to concentrate on. You may have misjudged a situation or you may have taken some kind of wrong road recently, therefore give a bit of thought to what you are trying to do with your life and where you must go from here on. You may be irritated with yourself for being foolish in some way. Eclipses can be quite difficult to live with for a while.

THURSDAY, 29TH JULY
Moon square Saturn

Someone in your family may feel rather neglected or ignored at the moment. If you've wondered why there's been a stony atmosphere around the home, and that sulks and long-drawn-out sighs are too common for comfort, here's your explanation! Take some time to show that you really do care. You can solve all sorts of domestic problems with a display of kindness and affection now.

FRIDAY, 30TH JULY
Sun trine Pluto

You are going to find yourself in a dominant position no matter whom you deal with today. Those around you, partners, friends and relative strangers will look to you for guidance and leadership especially in sticky social situations.

SATURDAY, 31ST JULY
Mercury into Cancer retrograde

Mercury's return to your Solar house of health and habits may be a hint to take a good look at your physical well-being. This would be a good time to get yourself checked over, from teeth to toenails just to make sure that everything's in fine working order.

August at a Glance

LOVE	❤	❤	❤	❤
WORK	★			
MONEY	£	£	£	
HEALTH	✚	✚	✚	✚
LUCK	⊌	⊌		

SUNDAY, 1ST AUGUST
Moon trine Mercury

It's a good day for making solid progress on the career front. You can project an image of someone who gets things done. Your efforts will find favour with those who are important now. Those of you who are out of a job may find that an opportunity occurring today will solve your problems.

MONDAY, 2ND AUGUST
Moon trine Sun

The message of the stars is one of hope especially for communications in your close relationship. You'll rarely find yourself more in tune with your other half so try to keep the conversation flowing because this should help to sort out any recent problems.

TUESDAY, 3RD AUGUST
Venus trine Jupiter

Domestic life may not be an arena for calm simplicity, but it will be the setting for some stunning strokes of luck as Venus and Jupiter, the two most fortunate planets, team up to increase the prosperity of you and yours!

WEDNESDAY, 4TH AUGUST
Moon trine Venus

A truly romantic interlude could turn into real passion today. You seem to have the kind of magnetic charisma that's guaranteed to make you irresistible to the opposite sex. Even if all you end up doing is sitting about at home with your loved one, make this as sexy and loving an occasion as you can. Set the scene with perfume, dim lights and sexy music on the magic music machine tonight!

AQUARIUS

THURSDAY, 5TH AUGUST
Moon conjunct Saturn

If there's the slightest thing wrong in your home you'll react like a drill sergeant-major bawling out the offender and getting your family to toe the line. The combined influence of the Moon and Saturn make you a stickler for detail and no stranger to hard work. Not for you a sloppy domestic scene. There may be a motive in all this attention to cleanliness and good order... perhaps the visit of an elderly relative is imminent?

FRIDAY, 6TH AUGUST
Mercury direct

You should feel less on edge and generally more healthy as Mercury gets back into his proper course from today. Apart from that a friend may be applying pressure to get you to do something that you're not at all keen on. Fortunately Mercury's forward motion should ensure that you have the eloquence to defuse the situation without ruffling any feathers.

SATURDAY, 7TH AUGUST
Sun square Mars

Jealousy often comes from unexpected sources. It's worse when people you know and trust openly express envy because you are getting on in life. Of course, there is the possibility that you're being a little too big for your boots, so adjust your attitude to them, and they'll adjust theirs to you. This need not be an ongoing problem.

SUNDAY, 8TH AUGUST
Sun opposite Uranus

The expectations of others are rather heavy today, especially since you tend to be in a rebellious, independent mood. You can't see any reason why you should simply fall in with anyone else's plans or desires, no matter how insistent they are. In fact, you'll be far more inclined to dig your heels in and do nothing rather than meekly toe the line.

MONDAY, 9TH AUGUST
Moon sextile Saturn

A day for hard work around the home is indicated by today's stars. There's a lot to be done, and you're just the right person to do it all! The tasks ahead may be daunting to lesser souls, but you are capable of anything!

AQUARIUS

TUESDAY, 10TH AUGUST
Sun square Saturn

Your mood is something like a roller-coaster ride at the moment. One minute you're on top of the world, the next in a pit of despair. It's unfortunate that the gloomier side tends to predominate today since the Sun makes a hard aspect to Saturn showing you just how much you've got to do before you can relax in either your present relationship or in your home. Don't be too down-hearted because persistence will pay off.

WEDNESDAY, 11TH AUGUST
New Moon eclipse

Though Nostradamus predicted the end of the world for this day, we are not so ambitious! Today's eclipse marks a major turning point in your life and this should turn your relationships inside out. If you are heavily influenced by other signs or planets, then the changes which are whirling around in your life may affect some other area of your life rather than the partnership one. However, others can expect a real make-or-break atmosphere in your love life now.

THURSDAY, 12TH AUGUST
Mercury into Leo

Mercury moves into the area of your chart which is concerned with relationships that are open and above-board now. This suggests that over the next few weeks you will have nothing to be secretive about in connection with your relationships with others. Your friendships will be free and easy and your lovers the kind whom you can happily take home to mother!

FRIDAY, 13TH AUGUST
Mercury opposite Neptune

I'm afraid that the brain will not be functioning at its best today. The logic of Mercury is fogged by the confusions of Neptune, especially where relationship are concerned. You may have mixed-up feelings or, it may be that you just can't express yourself properly to your other half.

SATURDAY, 14TH AUGUST
Mars opposite Saturn

It's likely to be a difficult day with a lot of pressure placed upon you. If you left alone organized you could get through a mountain of tasks but the chances are that no sooner have you started one than you'll be dragged off to another. You'll have to put your foot down if you are to finish anything.

AQUARIUS

SUNDAY, 15TH AUGUST
Venus into Leo retrograde

Relationships move to the forefront of your mind as Venus, planet of love re-enters her own solar house from today. Troublesome disputes and unruly emotions can now be faced in an open manner. There may be a sudden outburst of feeling but this is a good thing since it will clear the air.

MONDAY, 16TH AUGUST
Moon sextile Sun

You have a longing for far-off, exotic places but going on your own won't be much fun. You need someone around you to share an adventure now. However, if you are on your own go anyway. You'll find someone to be with when you get to wherever you're going!

TUESDAY, 17TH AUGUST
Mercury square Jupiter

An extremely unwelcome bill is about to land on your doorstep! The trouble is that you are unlikely to be the one that has run it up! Paying this expense is going to cause ructions in the home.

WEDNESDAY, 18TH AUGUST
Moon opposite Saturn

You may find it hard to cope with all the pressures that are being placed upon you at the moment. You may want to spend more time with your family, just when the demands of your job are getting heavier.

THURSDAY, 19TH AUGUST
Pluto direct

Your interest will be caught by wider world issues today. A small item of news could carry a message of transformation for your life. You'll be so moved that you'll want to do your own small bit for the benefit of others. An act of protest could convince you of the possibility of true justice. You may decide to involve yourself in politics or a special interest group. You need to actively contribute some of your efforts now.

FRIDAY, 20TH AUGUST
Sun conjunct Venus

This should be a great day and, hopefully, the start of a wonderful period. There will be plenty of togetherness between you and those whom you love and also an atmosphere of happy harmony all around you. Love is all important to you now and, whether you are at the start of a new attraction, or whether you are in the throes of an ongoing affair, enjoy every minute of it now.

SATURDAY, 21ST AUGUST
Moon trine Venus

The events of the day should prove what a good friend you are. Past favours stand you in good stead as both friends and family rally round to express their affection and gratitude. You're in an affable and outgoing mood so you'll be happy to see so many familiar faces on what promises to be a highly social day.

SUNDAY, 22ND AUGUST
Moon trine Jupiter

Your home and domestic circumstances are really rather good at present, and whatever you have in mind for yourself and your family will go particularly well today. You may be keen to move house now or to put an existing home into some kind of order, and it looks as though the opportunity to do this is fast approaching.

MONDAY, 23RD AUGUST
Sun into Virgo

Today, the Sun enters your Solar eighth house of beginnings and endings. Thus, over the next month, you can expect something to wind its way to a conclusion, while something else starts to take its place. This doesn't seem to signify a major turning point or any really big event in your life but it does mark one of those small turning points that we all go through from time to time.

TUESDAY, 24TH AUGUST
Venus square Mars

This is going to be a difficult day because it becomes increasingly obvious that your life is more tangled than a bowl of spaghetti. Your career seems at odds with the domestic situation, which in turn complicates affairs of the heart. You may feel like a juggler trying to keep too many balls in the air at once. To handle this situation you need delicacy and tact – so I should start practising if I were you!

WEDNESDAY, 25TH AUGUST
Jupiter retrograde

Jupiter turns to retrograde motion today and it will continue to move backwards in your chart for a few weeks to come. This will bring a slowing down in all domestic and family matters and it may also bring more expense in these areas than you had anticipated.

THURSDAY, 26TH AUGUST
Full Moon

Today's full Moon seems to be highlighting a minor problem in connection with financial matters today. You may have been overspending recently and this could be the cause of your current financial embarrassment but there does seem to be something deeper to be considered here. Perhaps the firm you work for has a temporary problem or maybe your partner is a bit short of cash just now.

FRIDAY, 27TH AUGUST
Mercury conjunct Venus

Words of love will be flowing all around you now. Your lover may surprise you by suggesting a romantic evening out or by bringing you tickets to a show, a musical, or a sporting event.

SATURDAY, 28TH AUGUST
Sun trine Jupiter

Your partner, your close associates and your closest allies will see eye to eye with you today and they may even be on hand to help you out of a domestic crisis or two. You will probably buy some kind of new item for the home now, and you will have to ask another family member to help you put it exactly where you want it to be.

SUNDAY, 29TH AUGUST
Moon trine Pluto

You may feel rather confused about all the recent changes that have occurred in your life. You are still reassessing your viewpoint but this needn't be a solitary activity. A good talk with an understanding friend will go a long way to clarifying your thoughts.

MONDAY, 30TH AUGUST
Saturn retrograde

All your domestic plans seem to be slowing down at the moment. If, for example, you are looking for a new home, then this will all go rather slowly from now on. Later in the year, all this will pick up once again.

TUESDAY, 31ST AUGUST
Mercury into Virgo

Mercury moves into one of the most sensitive areas of your chart from today. Anything of an intimate nature from your physical relationships to the state of your bank balance comes under scrutiny now. Turn your heightened perceptions to your love life, important partnerships, and any affair that deals with investment, insurance, tax or shared resources. An intelligent approach now will save you a lot of problems later.

September at a Glance

LOVE	♥	♥	♥	♥	♥
WORK	★	★	★		
MONEY	£	£			
HEALTH	☉	☉	☉		
LUCK	♘	♘			

WEDNESDAY, 1ST SEPTEMBER
Moon square Venus

There is evidence of tensions and awkwardness arising in the area of your home and family today and it seems to be the female members of your circle that are most likely to be at odds with each other. If you have a daughter or a mother, try not to allow them to wind you up, but stay calm and help them in their turn to take a calm and practical attitude to their problems.

THURSDAY, 2ND SEPTEMBER
Mars into Sagittarius

Friends are likely to be a strong influence on you at this time. Old friends may have interesting ideas to put your way, while new ones could come crowding into your life quite quickly now. You may join some kind of very active group who share your interests and are keen to have you as part of their organization. This may have something to do with sports or some other kind of energetic or outdoor activity.

FRIDAY, 3RD SEPTEMBER
Mercury trine Jupiter

This is a great time to look for a new home or to make arrangements to alter or improve your present one. Money seems to be easy to come by just now, especially in connection with property matters. There could be some extra funds coming your way through a family member or a through a close personal relationship.

AQUARIUS

SATURDAY, 4TH SEPTEMBER
Mercury square Pluto

Disturbing news heralds a big change in your life now. A friend may be the bearer of bad tidings, or you hear of a sadness that effects someone you're fond of. Try not to over-react. You're best bet is to be cool and calm now. After all, panicking won't help anyone and you need to know the full facts before you take any action. At least others know that you'll always provide a shoulder to cry on.

SUNDAY, 5TH SEPTEMBER
Moon sextile Saturn

Home-based work is favoured under the influence of the Moon and Saturn. You may wish to improve your environment, redecorate or just give the place a good going over. You'll be justifiably pleased by the results of your efforts.

MONDAY, 6TH SEPTEMBER
Mars sextile Neptune

An active social scene is forecast for today. Male friends especially will be very attentive and you'll find this very flattering. A sporting event or an exciting party could be on offer.

TUESDAY, 7TH SEPTEMBER
Moon opposite Uranus

When it comes to marriage or other close links, there are times when each partner needs their own space. That's the case today when duty and independence find themselves in opposition, much the Moon and Uranus. There's no need to cause ill-feeling by going your own way for a while; all that's needed is some openness and honesty. Then everyone concerned will know where they stand.

WEDNESDAY, 8TH SEPTEMBER
Sun conjunct Mercury

Approach contracts and agreements with caution today. That's not to say that they are bad things to get involved with, just that you've got to play your cards close to your chest to make the most of them. You have the ability to handle any negotiations with ease since your shrewd appreciation of realities gives you the edge over any opponents. You'll have no trouble with small print.

THURSDAY, 9TH SEPTEMBER
New Moon

Apart from a new Moon today, there are no major planetary happenings. This suggests that you avoid making major changes in your life just now but make a couple of fresh starts in very minor matters. You may feel like taking your partner to task over some irritating ways, but perhaps today is not the best day for doing this.

FRIDAY, 10TH SEPTEMBER
Sun trine Saturn

A serious turn of mind today. The Sun is in aspect to Saturn which makes you a sober, more practical sort of person than you've been of late. If you are considering a house move or alterations to your existing home, then it's a good time to get down to the nitty-gritty and sort out detailed information concerning loans and mortgages. When it comes to minor domestic expenses you demand quality and value.

SATURDAY, 11TH SEPTEMBER
Venus direct

At last Venus, planet of love, starts to behave herself, and since this occurs in your relationship area all affairs of the heart should now improve. Partnerships, both personal and business, will benefit from a renewed sense of co-operation.

SUNDAY, 12TH SEPTEMBER
Moon sextile Venus

Sometimes you just know when you need a vacation! It won't take much to convince you that it is time to pack your bags and head for the wide blue yonder and, if your partner shares your desire, then this idea becomes irresistible.

MONDAY, 13TH SEPTEMBER
Moon square Neptune

You'll be inclined to day-dream today. We all need that now and again I know, but when it's in company time you can expect a ticking off from your superiors for dereliction of duty. You have been warned!

TUESDAY, 14TH SEPTEMBER
Moon opposite Saturn

You seem to be under a good deal of pressure at the moment both at home and at work. You may be in one place while feeling that you really ought to be in another and that work is piling up all around you, wherever you may be.

AQUARIUS

WEDNESDAY, 15TH SEPTEMBER
Mars conjunct Pluto

You will be concerned with profound reviews on friendships and relationships at work and your social life in general will come under scrutiny. Mars makes a conjunction with Pluto today revealing an intense change in the way you look at your friendships, You could make changes in this area for the better which means some acquaintances could go by the way to make way for new ones. If so, so be it.

THURSDAY, 16TH SEPTEMBER
Mercury into Libra

Mercury enters your solar house of adventure on philosophy from today and stimulates your curiosity. Everything from international affairs to religious questions will tax your mind. Your desire to travel will be boosted for a few weeks, as indeed will a need to expand your knowledge, perhaps by taking up a course at a local college. Keep an open mind. Allow yourself encounters with new ideas.

FRIDAY, 17TH SEPTEMBER
Mercury trine Neptune

You could happily dream today away for the aspect between Mercury and Neptune puts your thoughts and desires so much in tune that you could be lost in a romantic reverie for much of the time. Instinctively you'll be aware that there isn't one of you aspirations that's beyond the bounds of possibility. Of course you will have to put some effort into attaining them but there's no harm in setting your sights on where you want to go now.

SATURDAY, 18TH SEPTEMBER
Moon square Mercury

Your emotions will cloud your judgement today and you may act on some kind of silly impulse. Don't worry about this and don't regret it because your intuitive urge may turn out to be more right than you first judged it to be.

SUNDAY, 19TH SEPTEMBER
Moon trine Saturn

The company of an elderly relative or friend will be pleasurable today. Possibly you will discover something fascinating from your own, or your family's past.

MONDAY, 20TH SEPTEMBER
Moon trine Sun

Today you just know that you are right! Your confidence will be on a real high and you will be absolutely sure that you are on the right track. A romance or relationship will begin to move into a much better mode now and you have a real chance of sorting out any misunderstandings that have arisen between you. You will be able to explain how you feel to your lover, and you will have an almost psychic understanding of his or her needs.

TUESDAY, 21ST SEPTEMBER
Mercury sextile Pluto

You're in quite a philosophical mood today ready and able to discuss the most profound concepts in depth. A person of like mind will be a pleasure to talk to and will come up with a few notions that will give you food for thought.

WEDNESDAY, 22ND SEPTEMBER
Moon opposite Venus

Mind what you say today! Other people, and this includes your nearest and dearest, will be tense and touchy and apt to blow up at the slightest hint of criticism. Your personal relationships could be going through a somewhat difficult time just now and you will need the world of patience in order to get through this phase.

THURSDAY, 23RD SEPTEMBER
Sun into Libra

The Sun moves into your Solar ninth house today and it will stay there for a month. This would be a good time to travel overseas or to explore new neighbourhoods. It is also a good time to take up an interest in spiritual matters. You may find yourself keen to read about religious or philosophical subjects or even to explore the world of psychic healing over the next month or so.

FRIDAY, 24TH SEPTEMBER
Mars sextile Uranus

Your friends will be amazed by the amount of fire and passion you can inject into any gathering. You may even make a speech! Rallying the troops and instilling them with a revolutionary fervour is the main feature of the day!

SATURDAY, 25TH SEPTEMBER
Full Moon

This is likely to be a really awkward day for any kind of travelling. A vehicle could let you down just when you most need it or the public transport that you usually rely on could suddenly disappear from the face of the earth.

AQUARIUS

SUNDAY, 26TH SEPTEMBER
Moon opposite Mercury

Your wonderfully logical, practical and sensible brain is on strike today. You will just not be able to think straight or to come up with a sensible answer to anything today, so don't try. Leave any important decisions until the stars have moved into a better position for the time being. In particular, it is not a good day to sign any important documents.

MONDAY, 27TH SEPTEMBER
Moon square Neptune

Sometimes you can't please anyone no matter how hard you try. Family loyalties are strained because relatives are a source of constant irritation since they seem determined to undermine your confidence and purposely misunderstand your every motive. You may have to deal with an elderly relation who makes an art out of awkwardness. Try to retain your patience.

TUESDAY, 28TH SEPTEMBER
Moon conjunct Saturn

A serious-minded attitude takes hold as the Moon conjuncts Saturn today. Old memories tinged with sadness rise to the surface but you'll be left with the conviction that you can make the future better. Dealings with your family, which may be depressing will actually solve some problems. Don't shy away from difficulty today because you can resolve things once and for all.

WEDNESDAY, 29TH SEPTEMBER
Moon trine Neptune

The events of the day will prove that a lot of those things that you've taken for granted, perhaps for years are falling away from you now. The Moon's aspect to Neptune encourages you to trust to your instincts and follow a course that isn't totally reliant on observable facts. This is particularly true of all creative ventures and in the area of romance. An infatuation is on the cards for many.

THURSDAY, 30TH SEPTEMBER
Moon trine Uranus

If you're a person who has always been sure about rights and wrongs, taste and decorum, you could be in for something of a shock today. Your eyes are now opened to other possibilities so some of your well-established views will undergo a swift review. Don't cling to conventions because this opening of your mind is a sign of your personal evolution.

October at a Glance

LOVE	♥				
WORK	★	★	★	★	★
MONEY	£	£			
HEALTH	☉	☉	☉		
LUCK	U	U	U	U	

FRIDAY, 1ST OCTOBER
Sun sextile Pluto

A hope that you've had for some time will take a step nearer to fulfilment today. You may have to keep this chance quiet for a while, but eventually all will be revealed and then you'll have a cause to celebrate.

SATURDAY, 2ND OCTOBER
Mercury sextile Venus

You would do well to talk over your beliefs and your personal philosophy of life with your partner today. You would also benefit by finding out what your loved ones think about these subjects. You may have to choose between religion and love at this time but there really doesn't seem to be much contest here because your feeling will outweigh your beliefs – just.

SUNDAY, 3RD OCTOBER
Moon square Mercury

Don't be too hard on yourself today. Accept that you have probably been working hard or that you have been under too much stress for your own good. Nobody can do everything and you are not superman (or superwoman, for that matter) so you shouldn't expect so much of yourself. You may have to spend some time with a colleague who is going through a crisis today.

MONDAY, 4TH OCTOBER
Moon sextile Sun

You feel centred, happy and at peace with the world today and other people are as happy with you as you are with yourself. This is an excellent time to speak with in-laws and relatives because they will understand your point of view.

AQUARIUS

TUESDAY, 5TH OCTOBER
Mercury into Scorpio

There's a certain flexibility entering your career structure as indicated by the presence of Mercury in your Solar area of ambition from today. You can now turn your acute mind to all sorts of career problems and solve them to everyone's satisfaction, and your own personal advantage. Your powers of persuasion will be heightened from now on, ensuring that you charm bosses and employers to get your own way. If seeking work, you should attend interviews because your personality will shine.

WEDNESDAY, 6TH OCTOBER
Sun trine Uranus

You could well ruin any idea that you were a stick-in-the-mud today. The Sun unites with Uranus to open your eyes and mind to the numerous possibilities surrounding you. Your thoughts will tend to the more unconventional and original. If you're artistically inclined, then there's an air of genius about you now. You may come across someone whose views you don't share but with whom you achieve a remarkable understanding.

THURSDAY, 7TH OCTOBER
Venus into Virgo

Venus enters the area of your chart that is closely involved with love and sex today. Oddly enough, this aspect can bring the end of a difficult relationship or, just as easily begin a wonderful new one. If you have been dating but haven't yet got around to 'mating', this could be the start of something wonderful. Your emotional life over the next two or three weeks should be something to remember, that's for sure!

FRIDAY, 8TH OCTOBER
Moon trine Neptune

You're obviously in an adventurous frame of mind today. The Moon and Neptune urge you to explore some obscure byways in the search for truth. Not only that, you'll be more than willing to provoke debate by taking an unconventional stance. Principles are the most important thing to you now, so being bogged down in mere practicalities isn't your scene at all.

SATURDAY, 9TH OCTOBER
New Moon

The New Moon in your house of adventure urges you to push ahead with new projects. You're in a self-confident mood, and feel able to tackle anything the world throws at you. There's a lure of the exotic today as well, as far-off place exert a powerful attraction. Think again about widening your personal horizons by travel or, indeed, by taking up an educational course. Intellectually you're on top form and your curiosity is boundless.

SUNDAY, 10TH OCTOBER
Venus trine Jupiter

The fortunes of both yourself and your family as a whole are set to improve under the rays of Jupiter and Venus. These fortunate planets have a strong influence of domestic harmony and happiness. There may also be the prospect of more money coming in!

MONDAY, 11TH OCTOBER
Jupiter square Neptune

You will feel a vague unease around family members today. You may need some time on your own, and should make sure that you get some. Family pressures and problems will be ever-present at the moment but at least you can ponder them in peace and quiet.

TUESDAY, 12TH OCTOBER
Void Moon

This is not a great day in which to decide anything or to start anything new. A void Moon suggests that there are no major planetary aspects being made, either between planets or involving the Sun or the Moon. This is a fairly unusual situation but it does happen from time to time and the only way to deal with it is to stick to your usual routines and do nothing special for a while.

WEDNESDAY, 13TH OCTOBER
Mercury square Uranus

Disturbing news today could put you in a panic, but the situation probably isn't as dire as you imagine! Don't over-react now! Just wait until the situation becomes clearer.

THURSDAY, 14TH OCTOBER
Neptune direct

Neptune goes into direct motion from today which helps your powers of concentration. You are more able to get important matters into perspective from now on. Any personal impulses that you've concealed for fear of seeming silly or weak-willed can now be admitted. You can show your innate sensitivity without worrying that others will make fun of your feelings.

AQUARIUS

FRIDAY, 15TH OCTOBER
Moon conjunct Mars

Lonely ladies who are reading this have a terrific opportunity of meeting someone new today and it would happen in the most unexpected way. The rest of you can enjoy sporting activities or anything that you do with friends in a group or a social setting. Therefore, phone your friends and suggest a game of golf or something similar.

SATURDAY, 16TH OCTOBER
Mercury opposite Saturn

If you feel at all tongue-tied and confused today you can put the blame on Mercury's opposition to Saturn which ties your thinking processes in knots. Irritations at home spill over into your professional life and you'll find that you can't concentrate on the job in hand. One think at a time! If some domestic issues need sorting out then act at once because they'll dominate your thoughts until they're resolved.

SUNDAY, 17TH OCTOBER
Mars into Capricorn

You seem to be entering a placid and peaceful backwater just now because Mars is disappearing into the quietest area of your chart. However, this is not quiet true because you will spend this reflective time working out what you want from life and also making preparations for your future. This is a good time to repay any loans or to fulfil any outstanding obligations towards others.

MONDAY, 18TH OCTOBER
Venus square Pluto

Hold back; don't rush into anything today! There seem to be wheels operating within wheels around you now and you are too embroiled in the middle of it all to see things clearly. Women may behave in a particularly manipulative manner, and you may never really be able to work out what is true and what isn't. Don't take anything on face value and don't let others wind you up.

TUESDAY, 19TH OCTOBER
Moon square Saturn

You may be keen to get out and about but circumstances may conspire to keep you indoors today. Your parents may need a bit of your help now and, if you do manage to get out of your home, it could be only to finish the day in their home instead. You can't win today.

W E D N E S D A Y , 2 0 T H O C T O B E R
Moon sextile Jupiter

Moneywise and in dealings with authority you're in luck today. A marvellous astral combination ensures that you won't take the less than perfect and are forceful and assertive. Just make sure that you don't take this wilfulness too far otherwise you could end up dishing out far more than anyone deserves. At least you are going to get what you want.

T H U R S D A Y , 2 1 S T O C T O B E R
Moon opposite Venus

You may want to be the last of the big spenders today but it is not really a good idea. You may need to consult an accountant or your bank manager in order to see what you can or cannot get away with during the months ahead. There is no doubt about it, whether you have only yourself to answer to or whether you are part of any kind of partnership, you will have to cut down on the luxuries for a while.

F R I D A Y , 2 2 N D O C T O B E R
Sun square Neptune

Self-confidence is a casualty of a harsh aspect between the Sun and Neptune today. In career affairs especially you'll be wondering whether your past decisions were the right ones. You're prone to a lot of confusion today and aims that you once cherished will be questioned now. You may be the victim of a deceptive influence in work so don't take anything on face value just now.

S A T U R D A Y , 2 3 R D O C T O B E R
Sun into Scorpio

The Sun moves decisively into your horoscope area of ambition from today bringing in a month when your worldly progress will achieve absolute priority. You need to feel that what you are doing is worthwhile and has more meaning than simply paying the bills. You may feel the urge to change you career, to make a long-term commitment to a worthwhile cause, or simply to demand recognition for past efforts. However this ambitious phase manifests you can be sure that your prospects are considerably boosted from now on.

S U N D A Y , 2 4 T H O C T O B E R
Full Moon

The Full Moon today focuses firmly on family and domestic issues. Perhaps it's time for some straight talking because this is the best opportunity you'll get to put an end to home-based or emotional problems. In some ways it's time to put your cards on the table, yet equally to give credit and take some share of blame in family affairs. Apart from such personal concerns it's time to speak to someone in authority about your ambitions.

MONDAY, 25TH OCTOBER
Venus trine Saturn

Thrift and economy are the watchwords today, even though your financial fortunes are looking reasonably good at the moment. Just because some extra cash is likely to come in doesn't mean that you should immediately splash it all out again! Be sensible and budget carefully!

TUESDAY, 26TH OCTOBER
Moon opposite Mercury

You may not be able to think straight today and you could get yourself into something of a muddle either at home or at work. The trick to surviving this kind of planetary aspect is to keep to the most mundane and routine of tasks and to take plenty of breaks. Don't bother with anything that requires acuity or clarity of mind until the stars have moved on a bit.

WEDNESDAY, 27TH OCTOBER
Moon opposite Pluto

When you decide to dig your heels in, there's very little that can shift you from your position. So, when those around you press you for an instant decision today, you'll be less than inclined to oblige them. You may feel some resentment or envy just now, so long-term decisions aren't a good idea anyway. Go by your instincts now, and wait until your mind is less clouded by negative emotion.

THURSDAY, 28TH OCTOBER
Mercury sextile Neptune

f ever there was a day when you should leap up and shout 'Eureka' this is it! The combination of Mercury and Neptune inspires you with the most amazing flashes of intuition. Don't ignore your hunches now. You may even experience a prophetic dream. It doesn't matter how you rationalize it, just follow the good advice that you're being psychically urged to take.

FRIDAY, 29TH OCTOBER
Moon opposite Mars

People at work seem to take a delight in being perverse today. Nothing seems to please them and, no matter how well a job is being done, they're bound to find fault with something. Blowing your top will only make matters worse so expend some of that furious energy you stir up in some vigorous exercise. You've got to find some way to burn off your irritation otherwise you'll end up with all sorts of little ailments that can be traced directly to stress.

SATURDAY, 30TH OCTOBER
Mercury into Sagittarius

The swift-moving planet Mercury enters your eleventh Solar house today and gives a remarkable uplift to your social prospects. During the next few weeks you'll find yourself at the centre point of friendly interactions. People will seek you out for the pleasure of your company. It's also a good time to get in contact with distant friends and those you haven't seen for a while. The only fly in the ointment is that you shouldn't expect a small phone bill.

SUNDAY, 31ST OCTOBER
Moon square Sun

Some peace and quiet is the order of the day… If, that is, you can find some. There are still a lot of demands made upon you but you need some time to yourself, perhaps engaged in a favourite hobby to refresh your spirit. Too much interference from others will only result in you losing your temper. Put up a 'Do Not Disturb' sign, you'll feel better for a little solitude.

November at a Glance

LOVE	❤	❤	❤		
WORK	★	★	★	★	★
MONEY	£	£	£		
HEALTH	✛				
LUCK	♘	♘			

MONDAY, 1ST NOVEMBER
Void Moon

Today is one of those odd days when there are no important planetary aspects being made, not even to the Moon. The best way to tackle these kinds of days is to stick to your usual routine and to avoid starting anything new or tackling anything of major importance. If you do decide to do something large today, then it will take longer and be harder to cope with than it would normally.

TUESDAY, 2ND NOVEMBER
Moon square Mercury

It's a very confusing day on most fronts when your mental processes are slowed down and clouded by the Moon's influence. Red tape, documents, and official correspondence will leave you paralysed with indecision. All you want to do is escape and possibly ask a friend to help out, unfortunately that won't do much good, since friends are as confused as you are. This is not a good day to deal with far-reaching business or financial affairs anyway so try to put them off.

WEDNESDAY, 3RD NOVEMBER
Moon trine Saturn

Your parents could help you out in a big way today. They may be happy to lend you something that you need or to come and give a hand with any household problem. People in positions of responsibility will be quite impressed by your intelligence and your ability today too.

THURSDAY, 4TH NOVEMBER
Moon sextile Mercury

You're terribly restless today and can't wait to get away from the jaded and familiar. Though your basic inclinations may be to travel as far away as you can, you'd be the first to admit that it's not always possible. If you are chained to the domestic or work scene then you need something to take your mind off the usual affairs of your life. A good conversation, a fascinating book or absorbing TV show should improve your mood.

FRIDAY, 5TH NOVEMBER
Moon trine Uranus

You've had enough of the well-worn pathways of your life by now so it would be a good idea to follow the lead provided by the Moon and Uranus and take some time out to explore some new avenues. I'm not talking about work or family issues, this is to do with your own self-satisfaction. Find out more about a subject that interests you or visit somewhere new. You need to stretch your mental boundaries now.

SATURDAY, 6TH NOVEMBER
Sun opposite Saturn

It would be too easy to give in to pessimism today. Any negative thoughts would be self-defeating. The trouble is that the pressure is on both at work and in the home. Criticism you receive will strike hard, but try not to let it get you down. Make an extra effort to be cheerful.

SUNDAY, 7TH NOVEMBER
Sun sextile Mars

In the career stakes good fortune is with you, though it won't hurt to give it a helping hand. The Solar aspect to Mars makes it plain that you can achieve great things now, but you can maximize your chances by thinking your moves through carefully. Strategy is the key to success in all ventures now. Try not to be too underhanded though. You are going to win so there's no need for over-kill.

MONDAY, 8TH NOVEMBER
New Moon

The new Moon today shows the great heights that you could possibly attain. The message is that there's nothing to fear except fear itself. Reach for the stars and you've got it made. Your career should begin to blossom now and you can achieve the kind of respect and status that you are looking for over the next month or so.

TUESDAY, 9TH NOVEMBER
Mercury into Scorpio

Your job will take precedence today and you must make an effort to get your voice heard. Fortunately, this will not be too difficult because your superiors and your colleagues will be reasonably ready to hear what you have to say. You may have some bright ideas in other areas of life today as well, and you shouldn't hesitate to put these into practice.

WEDNESDAY, 10TH NOVEMBER
Moon sextile Uranus

Though you tend to prefer the tried and true, you won't lose out if you look for a short cut today. Try some lateral thinking because all is not as it seems now. A friend or colleague may be helpful in pointing you in the right direction now. Don't be afraid to try something new because it's likely to be better than sticking to the old ways of doing things. Socially, you'll be attracted to a new venue.

THURSDAY, 11TH NOVEMBER
Moon trine Jupiter

There is a fresh wind blowing through your bank account now because there are new opportunities for money-making on the horizon. You should try to distance yourself from other people's problems, and you should also try to take a detached attitude to anything that is going on around you. There will be heartening news today, and this may be just the proof that you need to show others that you have been right in your thinking all along.

FRIDAY, 12TH NOVEMBER
Moon square Venus

Your mood today is philosophical and you would enjoy nothing better than to sit down with an intelligent pal and discuss the meaning of life, the movement of the Solar system, astrology and religion. However, practical matters have a nasty way of imposing themselves on you and preventing you from drifting and dreaming in the way you want. The washing-up calls you, the ironing is moaning at you from the corner of the room and the kids must be fed. Shame, isn't it?

SATURDAY, 13TH NOVEMBER
Moon conjunct Mars

You're keeping a lot of unexpressed frustration under control early on in the day, however internal pressure is building. It's no answer to keep negative feelings bottled up, but exploding in all directions isn't a good idea either. Direct your anger at the root cause of the problem, not take it out on all around you. You'll be tempted to plot an intricate and devastating revenge, but you should try to prove your detractors wrong by doing the best you can.

SUNDAY, 14TH NOVEMBER
Saturn square Uranus

A family member's rebellious attitudes will cause you to act like a tyrant today. It may be an over-reaction yet it is understandable given the nature of the rebellion!

MONDAY, 15TH NOVEMBER
Moon square Saturn

A scheme that you've cooked up might not win immediate approval from your family, but that's no reason to give it up completely. Some compromise is possible so with a little give and take anything is possible… if, that is, you can get them to listen.

TUESDAY, 16TH NOVEMBER
Mercury sextile Mars

Though there may be problems at work, you can defeat all opposition with a little forethought. The shrewdness of Mercury unites with the strategic cunning of Mars to enable you to run rings around any opponent.

AQUARIUS

WEDNESDAY, 17TH NOVEMBER
Venus sextile Pluto

A close friend may wish to get even closer under the intense influence of Pluto mixed in with the romantic vibes of Venus. This is fine if you're single and agreeable, but if there are relationship complications on either side then you'd be wise to think again before you get in too deep. You'll have to be firm yet tactful to get out of this without bruising tender feelings.

THURSDAY, 18TH NOVEMBER
Moon trine Mercury

The Lunar aspect to Mercury makes your mind extremely perceptive. Any secrets around you will be a secrets no longer, for you'll see through any deceit with little trouble. This should be an inspired day which brings out inner abilities that you didn't know existed. Financially too, your luck's in.

FRIDAY, 19TH NOVEMBER
Moon sextile Neptune

Like a bolt from the blue, a sudden inspiration will strike you today. Like the proverbial lightbulb, your brain will be illuminated by a brilliant idea! Now all you have to do is put it into practice!

SATURDAY, 20TH NOVEMBER
Venus trine Uranus

You feel the call of the new today. Venus's aspect to Uranus opens your mind to novel concepts and ingenious arguments. Unconventional people will now enter your life, and you'll find them more interesting and far less shocking than you'd have ever imagined. This influence could well rub off because you're in an eccentric mood yourself.

SUNDAY, 21ST NOVEMBER
Mars square Jupiter

You need to review your methods of communicating with others today. This may be something subtle, such as learning to listen to people rather than talking at them. On the other hand, this may be a simple matter of buying a new telephone or getting the office fax machine mended. You may need to sort out some kind of transport situation now too.

MONDAY, 22ND NOVEMBER
Sun into Sagittarius

As the Sun makes its yearly entrance into your eleventh Solar house, you can be sure that friends and acquaintances are going to have a powerful influence on your prospects. The Sun's harmonious angle to your own sign gives an optimism and vitality to your outgoing nature. Social life will increase in importance over the next month. You'll be a popular and much sought after person. Obstacles that have irritated you will now be swept away.

T U E S D A Y , 2 3 R D N O V E M B E R
Full Moon

Your creative soul and romantic yearnings come under the influence of today's Full Moon, so its time to take stock of those things in your life that no longer give any emotional satisfaction. Children and younger people may need a word or two of advice now and the love lives of all around you will become the centre of interest. You're own romantic prospects may see an upturn too.

W E D N E S D A Y , 2 4 T H N O V E M B E R
Moon trine Venus

This is not a day for duty. The Lunar aspect to Venus puts a romantic spark in your soul. There's nothing you'd like better than an intimate *tête-à-tête* with someone you love. Forget your worries for today at least and take that special person in your life out for a night of glamour. If you haven't got a special person, go for glamour anyway. Someone will catch your eye.

T H U R S D A Y , 2 5 T H N O V E M B E R
Sun sextile Neptune

The finer things in life have tremendous appeal today. The Sun makes a splendid aspect to Neptune putting you in touch with your inner self. Art, music and theatre are very important as a way of reaching a sense of beauty and truth that's so often lacking in day-to-day life. You truly show appreciation of the talents of others now, and maybe you can show that you too are a creative soul.

F R I D A Y , 2 6 T H N O V E M B E R
Mars into Aquarius

Mars enters your own sign of the zodiac today and it will spend a few weeks there, bringing zest, energy and a welcome element of fun into your life. You seem to be on a 'roll' at the moment and, as long as you keep up the momentum, there is no reason why you should not be able to reach your objectives.

S A T U R D A Y , 2 7 T H N O V E M B E R
Moon opposite Neptune

There's a lot of uncertainty around today especially in affairs of the heart. You want to know exactly where you stand but emotions by nature aren't going to yield up their complexities to analysis. A new relationship may seem too good to be true, but you can't work out whether you're being too cynical or not. Perhaps you're prone to suspicion now, if so try to cool down because it's hard to work anything out logically today.

SUNDAY, 28TH NOVEMBER
Moon square Mercury

If you want any peace now, you'd better keep your mouth firmly shut because you'll get very little sympathy or understanding now. The trouble is that you are pretty logical while those around you are too emotional to see anything rationally at all!

MONDAY, 29TH NOVEMBER
Mars conjunct Neptune

You will be putting your energies into helping others today. You may sacrifice your time, energy or money for the sake of those who are worse off than you are. You may experience some kind of strange psychic event such as a dream that foretells the future.

TUESDAY, 30TH NOVEMBER
Moon trine Saturn

Pressure from an older family member, possibly a mother or mother figure will keep you on the straight and narrow today. Advice about your personal relationships or your financial prospects will be forthcoming so be prepared to listen!

December at a Glance

LOVE	♥				
WORK	★	★	★	★	★
MONEY	£	£	£		
HEALTH	✚	✚			
LUCK	U	U	U		